# Go! Do the Same

*Developing Parish Outreach Programs*

Nancy Vendura, C.S.J.

Paulist Press

New York/Mahwah, N.J.

"It is like yeast which a woman took to knead into three measures of flour until the whole mass of dough began to rise."

(Lk 13:20-21)

Book design by Celine M. Allen.

Illustrations by Rosanna DeMarco.

Copyright © 1992 by the Sisters of St. Joseph, Brentwood, N.Y.

ISBN: 0-8091-3308-3

Published by Paulist Press
997 Macarthur Boulevard
Mahwah, New Jersey 07430

Printed and bound in the United States of America

# Contents

## Acknowledgments

"Thanks!" to God and to my parents who created me out of love and for love. "Thanks!" to the Double Family of St. Vincent de Paul and the Sisters of St. Joseph of Brentwood, New York for "making" me part of you and your charism part of me. "Thanks!" to my enabling and supportive pastor Msgr. Peter V. Kain who had a vision and who selected me to carve it out and see it through. "Thanks!" to some very special people, Arlene Rego, Patricia Mooney, CSJ, Rev. William Rueger, Rosanna DeMarco, Steven Aggugia and Rev. Thomas Pettei for sharing your time, energy, enthusiasm, and technical talents with me in the progressive stages of my authoring this book.

"Thanks!" to all of you with whom I have had the privilege of co-ministering. You have helped me to know the power of God who can achieve so much good when people work together to accomplish a shared vision. "Thanks!" to the countless people I have been so favored to serve in hospitals, schools, refugee camps, community agencies and parish churches. It is you in whom I have seen the face of God and from whom came the impetus and the courage to shape these pages.

Gratefully through this book I unite myself to all of you and "the neighbor" everywhere asking that the Holy Spirit of God blow where it will.

# Introduction

Outreach at Our Lady of Lourdes began in September 1985 with a small group of volunteers serving the sick in their homes. As the needs of the sick and their families became known, Our Lady of Lourdes began to reach out to other area needs. Basic life-support programs developed through Outreach to address people's legitimate needs for food, clothing, shelter, employment, care of single-parent children and financial aid.

Over a five year span 720 people—professional and non-professional men and women, teens and adults—have volunteered to assist the needy through Outreach. Over 204 area families with sick members have benefited from the volunteer assistance (personal care, shopping, house-cleaning, meal preparation) of Our Lady of Lourdes Outreach. The Food Program provides 8,677 meals annually and offers people other basic care. For some, there have been successful outcomes for employment and housing. More than 800 bereaved families have been touched by Outreach.

Awareness of local needs drew other church leaders together in a strong cooperative spirit. This ecumenical spirit remains supportive of the endeavors of Our Lady of Lourdes Outreach which reaches out without discrimination to assist the area's poor. In the spirit of the gospel, area churches endeavor to reflect "their neighbors'" needs to the local community and to elicit a compassionate response.

In cooperation with churches and area agencies, Outreach serves a vast variety of the neighborhood's needy. For all who present themselves in legitimate need, Outreach extends a "Welcome!" Outreach is people caring for people in response to the neighbor in need. Outreach is the love commandment made visible—Love your neighbor as yourself. "And who is the neighbor? The one who treats another with compassion."

Today people can and often do turn to various agencies and providers to help them when they are in need. Health problems are often addressed in doctors' offices, hospitals and clinics. At home, these needs are often furnished through visiting nurse services or through assistance from vendor agencies. People who have basic needs such as food, shelter or clothing can turn to private human service agencies. Some people benefit financially from government programs such as income maintenance, HEAP, WIC, food stamps, and more. So why would a local parish organize itself to assist people with such human needs? Do parish services to the needy merely duplicate services already available? Does a parish have something unique to offer its people? I believe the parish's compassionate approach to human life through all its stages is in itself a distinct and manifest invitation to God.

One woman, grieving the loss of her son, succinctly told me, "Sister, I've been seeing a psychiatrist for over one year now but to no avail. This is only my second time seeing you but I know without a doubt all will be well for me because here I have found something which I needed and which no one else has given me. Here, I have found God."

The gospel of Jesus commands love and service of neighbor. Jesus himself spent his life preaching the gospel, teaching and healing the blind, the sick and the lame. Through the ages, Christians aspired to do what Jesus did when he walked the earth.

Traditionally, priests regularly preach in parishes, the sacraments remain central to the life of the church, and parishes offer religious education to their members. Certainly we continue to believe that equally essential to the Christian church, local as well as universal, is that the people of God must care for one another as Jesus commanded. The local church/parish is the primary means of accomplishing Jesus' love mandate. Parishes can and must facilitate Christian service through creative program planning to help meet the social, health, interpersonal, and spiritual needs of its people. Parishes ought to organize people willing to care for "the neighbor."

This book intends to assist you, the reader, to reexamine and focus your personal resources and that of your worshiping community to the benefit of the people among you. What is written here is a short catechesis patterned on consciousness raising and Christian volunteerism deepened through compassionate service. This book invites individual Christians and all parishes to organize and welcome the neighbor in need. It hopes to awaken human and Christian sensibilities toward enabling the oppressed and helpless who come to a parish for assistance. These pages are hope-filled and will be a help to any parish which grapples with improving, organizing, and/or expanding the assistance of basic needs to the needy neighbor. Beyond the honest sharing of one parish's meager beginnings and its ultimate success story, the reader will learn how an entire Christian community can be strengthened in and bonded through faith by living out Jesus' mandate to love the neighbor through the concrete and spiritual enrichment of its people.

Keep in mind that the parish model presented here is distinct from any medical model, nursing model, social work model, or government model. The parish has its own unique holistic model of "delivering care" to its people; it is the mode of Christ's compassion.

The programs described herein are not circumscribed by circumstances of race, sex, age, creed or geography, viz., urban vs. rural. What is proposed here has been successfully implemented in an ethnically varied urban parish of 3,000 registered families. Because the applied principles are Christian and blend managerial and organizational skills with the psychology of helping professions, the programs described in this book can be appropriately and readily adapted to meet human needs wherever they are found. While the size and rate of growth of parish programs may be influenced by such variables as geography, sex, age, ethnicity, etc., the validity and effectiveness of the programs described in this book are reliable. The reader will find the following pages oriented toward self as Christian, possible program initiator, or overall program director. It is intended that pastors and parish leaders at large as well as pastoral students will discover in these pages that practical form and substance which can organize and advance their own parish vision of "servant church."

The material is simply organized. Each program has a section which projects the particular goal or aim of the cited program. The explicit description of the program's smooth design is a personal challenge to the reader to "go and do the same."

The chapters include actual outcomes described for the reader through selective testimony, case studies, letters from recipients, recorded commentary and statement, and general feedback information.

While independently presented for the purpose of clarity and the organization of material, the programs described in this book greatly influence and hinge upon each other for their own individual success and for the triumph of the whole.

Likewise, it is to be noted that although the programs described herein can be initiated and maintained by a coordinating individual, the absolute necessity of a director to oversee, synchronize, organize and integrate the interfacing of various program combinations cannot be denied.

# Foreword

Dear Reader,

I write this book as an encouragement to local churches everywhere who wish to initiate Christian service programs or engender parishioner participation in assisting "the neighbor."

What you will read is meant to be exciting. Each program described herein leaps beyond an imaginary vision into the actual consummation of Jesus' mandate to love God and to serve others.

Note the uncomplicated basis of the program planning explained here. Observe the simplicity of planning and the graduating growth of program organization toward final maturity and permanency. This book is intended to serve you, so feel free to lift and adapt the forms and procedures helpful to your own local parish and its people's needs. Choose a program or programs which can be realistically implemented in your parish. Begin with the program you perceive to be the most simple yet one that will be certain to address the needs of the people of your own parish.

I advise the reader to always remember that for best results all successful parish programs should begin very simply. Consistent and healthy program growth is fostered by decision making and planning based on gradual program development and implementation.

Read about, be inspired and be excited by the compassionate model of Christ explained in these pages. Then embrace the challenge: "Go! Do the same."

May these pages animate and strengthen you in God's service.

# Chapter 1
# Before Beginning

In the very beginning and before making any plans for program creation, it is wise to observe some points of reference which are the basis and foundation of realistic program planning. These "frames of reference" include:

    1. self-knowledge on the part of the potential Outreach parish program planner and/or for the person intending to directly provide service to the neighbor;

    2. theological concepts of Christian volunteerism and their application;

    3. practical psychological approaches to volunteer recruitment and maintenance.

**Self-Knowledge/Inventory**

The person coming to a parish intending to assist people in need should have a basic awareness of his or her personal abilities or strengths. One of the most important initial decisions an Outreach director must make and one upon which hangs the destiny of Outreach programs and their development is whether the director intends to direct program services vs. personally providing for people in need. Knowing the consequence of his or her choice will enable the director to knowingly steer program development toward success.

The Outreach director, for example, could choose to be a role model for volunteers by being a direct care provider for people in need. This decision to be primarily devoted to provide for and actually take care of the people (e.g. the homebound, the grieving, people needing food, shelter, or employment, walk-ins, etc.) would significantly limit the number of people to receive Outreach assistance.

On the other hand, as facilitator or enabler the director of Outreach might decide to concentrate time and energy in gathering volunteers from the parish, encouraging and assisting them to serve people in need. This latter approach would ensure larger program growth and a wider catechesis of volunteers. However, it is also notable and probably more satisfying for the Outreach director to converge the two above considerations for a mode of operation as direct care provider as well as facilitator and enabler. The final determination is important and should not be made in haste.

Before choosing to be a primary provider, deciding to facilitate and enable, or do both, it would be wise for the Outreach director to venture a self-inventory. This will help ensure a selection that will be both satisfying and productive not only in the earlier and quieter days of Outreach, but also later on when program growth significantly increases the workload.

Following are selected questions which can be used as a guide to an open and honest skills inventory. The inventory suggests skills appropriate to one considering either program planning (PP) and/or someone wanting to directly assist people in meeting their own needs by providing direct service (DS).

1. Is my strength organization (PP) or is it role modeling? (DS)
2. Am I good at program development? (PP)
3. Am I a listener or a supporter? (PP/DS)
4. Do I collaborate with people, with other agencies, with other churches? (PP/DS)
5. How am I as a supervisor? (PP)
6. Do I have interpersonal skills? (PP/DS)
7. Do I have any leadership training? (PP)
8. How spiritually strong am I to lead others to God? (PP/DS)
9. Do I have a background in teaching or counseling? (DS)
10. Do I have experience with curriculum planning or group facilitating? (PP)
11. Am I a nurse, a musician, an artist? (DS)
12. Do I have interviewing skills? (DS)

One must remember that because the Outreach "structure" is very fluid and flexible, the director of Outreach will meet a great variety of demands and needs. It is possible, therefore, for the Outreach director to use and to maximize any and all of his or her talents and gifts. For example a director with teaching skills can utilize his or her teaching expertise in helping people learn how to appropriately express themselves to area agencies and so obtain need entitlements or gain the benefit of emotional release. Someone with a strong nursing background will better understand those healthful or unhealthful adjustments of a person experiencing distress. A musically or artistically inclined director can use these talents to tap into and uplift the downtrodden or to soothe the anxious. Such talents help to inspire and evoke prayer for volunteers and also for people supporting Outreach programs.

Having invited the reader to make a choice that would give direction to the role of the Outreach director as provider or as director of services, a third and more realistic option exists. The director of Outreach can assume both roles simply by altering the percentage of time devoted to each.

For example, the Outreach director could give direct service for a small amount of time each week—say, home visiting for three or four hours a week—and with the remainder of time he or she could recruit and train volunteers and plan and direct programs. Perhaps the opposite ratio might better suit the time, talents, and tasks of the Outreach director and the Outreach program at large. For example, the Outreach director might decide to act as director and program planner primarily for two days a week. That would leave three days for him or her to provide direct service—e.g., going to the homes of the people or assisting individuals or families in the office.

## Christian Volunteerism

Outreach volunteers are the good Samaritans of today. They are significant, necessary and critical to Outreach and its vision because volunteers embody Christ's compassion by bringing love and tenderness to people, especially to the poor and downtrodden. Volunteers concretize the parish's philosophy, theology, spirit and practice of care and concern for people because volunteers make God real for others. By their accepting and non-critical care of the neighbor, volunteers impart Christ's mercy, compassion, forgiveness and healing to others. Yet volunteers are often unaware of the motivation and implication of their willing gift of self to others. Rather, offering to freely donate oneself to care for the needy neighbor through a church based program is often the wordless expression of a person's desire to be closer to God. Putting faith in action is a volunteer's "yes" to a God who calls him or her to further thought and prayer through Christian service. Volunteerism is thus a call to holiness and a challenge to "put on Christ" so as to live and model compassionate caring for people.

Volunteers are male and female, young and old. They are racially varied and sometimes come from different faiths. What draws them to service as volunteers reflects these differences. Some want to involve themselves in Outreach, thinking first and foremost of being a good Samaritan. Other people give their time and energy out of a sense of gratitude to God. Many volunteer to give their service primarily because of their own vivid personal memories of the experience of pain in life and their struggle to overcome conflict. Finally, and perhaps surprisingly, there are persons who may actually be suffering while concurrently offering to freely help others through the parish Outreach program. Such individuals may ache from boredom or from some family difficulty. Their distress may be over-challenging children, or they may be the "sandwich generation," caught between their husbands and children and an aging parent. Some come with serious financial concerns. Hurting people who volunteer while enduring the experience of personal pain are those who give from their own "want," like the poor woman in the gospel who gave her last penny. Volunteerism for such afflicted persons becomes perhaps the most Christian of all challenges, viz., to compassionately reach out to others through and while suffering as did the crucified and dying Christ.

One must realize that Christian volunteerism, while good in itself, is dead and lifeless except for a vehicle of expression. It is the Outreach director who can and must provide volunteers with viable, albeit flexible, service structures based on gospel values. While flexible vehicles, structures and channels are the means to an end, namely, service of the neighbor, they are also an end in themselves. People in need will experience the help of others as facilitated through an adaptable framework. At the same time, gospel-built structures and channels will be the practical pathway of support and guidance for volunteers. Volunteers will discover themselves buttressed and assisted by a framework that will:

(a) Encourage them to reflect upon their own personal motivation,

(b) Facilitate their expression of their own giftedness,

(c) Strengthen the awareness of the Christian and compassionate dimension of their service.

Thus it behooves the Outreach director to invest time and energy in the people who present themselves to a parish as its potential Outreach volunteers regardless of, but conscious of, their motives for donating themselves for the neighbor. In order for the director and potential volunteer to get to know more about each other and the philosophy and the expectations of Outreach, the Outreach director and potential volunteer should meet individually, face to face, for 45 to 60 minutes. This is a time for each to begin feeling comfortable with the other. It is a time for exploring people's motives for volunteering, and a time for imparting the call of Christ to be compassionate as is our heavenly Father.

## Philosophy/Theology

The initial meeting between director and potential volunteer should be informal and non-threatening. All information should be imparted in a comfortable, dialogical fashion, which calls for attentive listening. Punctuated silence allows thinking time for the volunteer and an opportunity for self-expression and the sharing of ideas. Introductions and an opening prayer help to set a relaxed climate. It is recommended that the director spend the first 20 minutes listening to the individual and his or her desires and expectations as a potential volunteer in the program. The director should be calm and unrushed, allowing time for the volunteer to tell something about himself or herself. Sensitive and gentle questioning and a guided conversation assist relaxation for potential volunteers. Who they are, where they live, their family and personal interests, should be important and engaging to the director. After 15 or 20 minutes of interested listening, most potential volunteers comfortably grow in their desire to have the director share his or her own thoughts and impressions. At this time potential volunteers should be commended for the goodness in them which impels the desire to give to others. Potential volunteers should be made aware that their self-offering to Outreach is God's way of calling them to be imitators of Christ.

The good Samaritan gospel story (Lk 10:25-37) is the overall philosophy of Outreach. The director can read and must explain this passage in detail to the volunteer. At least 20 minutes or so should be taken for this. Contrast the characteristics of Jesus' parable with contemporary examples. Emphasize that Outreach is this good Samaritan gospel story alive in today's world. It is important that the director explain for the potential volunteer that while St. Luke tells us that eventually some neighbor came to the assistance of a wounded and needy person, the helping neighbor, like *the Outreach volunteer, could not/cannot totally care for the injured person.* It will help the potential volunteer to know that like the good Samaritan in Jesus' parable, today's Outreach volunteer does what little is possible for the injured one, and then refers the person to an "innkeeper" (Outreach director and other volunteers) for further assistance. The Outreach volunteer does not take on full responsibility for the wounded person. Rather, stress the good Samaritan story which tells of cooperation and support between the neighbor (Outreach volunteer) and the innkeeper (director and other volunteers), who work together to heal and provide for the poor person, the victim of circumstances.

## Psychology/Expectation

During this initial time together, clarify Outreach's expectations. Remind each volunteer that his or her primary responsibility is to self and to family. Affirm that volunteerism should not take from family and personal priorities and that each should ponder and pray about the amount of time he or she wishes to donate. The Outreach director would profit by suggesting that the potential volunteer give less time than initially planned because initial enthusiasm may wane. Donations of time can always be increased at a later date when volunteers are usually more comfortable with their roles and their service to the neighbor, and the time/energy commitment involved.

## Psychology/Comfort

While people are generally comfortable with and usually appreciate giving time and energy to a cause for which they have some feeling, most people have two reservations about volunteering in a church program.

1. Many fear that the time they wish to give will eventually "snowball" into feeling that they will have to give more and more time to the church program. Often volunteers say they find it nearly impossible to say "no" to a personal request from the director or a coordinator especially if it is to do a good deed for a needy person, and they anticipate feelings of being overwhelmed and all-consumed by the needs of the people.

2. The second concern of volunteers is their belief that they will not be "up to the task." Many volunteers have the idea that they will not have the skills to "do the job" properly. They express concern that the director or the person served will not be satisfied with the quality or the amount of the work that is done.

Toward the end of the initial encounter, the Outreach director usually becomes aware of these real preoccupations which are deterrents to personal happiness and program success. The director must be sensitive and direct. Each volunteer should know that the volunteer time agreed upon will never escalate. The volunteer and the director then explore the task that the volunteer feels most comfortable performing, as well as the volunteer's time commitment. Once clear about the nature of time and task, firm assurance must be given to the volunteer that there will be no change unless desired by the volunteer. It is suggested that while in the volunteer's presence, the director record the volunteer donation of time and task. The Outreach Volunteer Reference Form (page 97) can facilitate the recording and organizing of volunteers. Before ending the meeting with a spontaneous prayer, the director assures the volunteer that no one—not the volunteer, not the director, nor the receiver of services—will independently alter the agreement.

For example, a volunteer gives one hour a week in assisting an elderly person with her meal preparation needs. The donation of the volunteer is one hour of time. The task to be accomplished is meal preparation. The elderly person asks the volunteer to stay an additional half hour or to come twice that week so that the volunteer can help with housekeeping. The volunteer, already instructed by the director, is empowered to inform the elderly person that the task cannot change from meal preparation to housekeeping nor can the one hour commitment be raised 30 minutes without the approval of the Outreach director. The volunteer instructs the elderly person and/or calls the Outreach director herself for guidance in this matter. If the elderly person's need is legitimate, the informed Outreach director has the option of (1) assigning a second volunteer to the home of the elderly person to do the task of housekeeping or (2) approving the expanded volunteerism for the meal preparation volunteer, only in agreement with and upon the suggestion of this volunteer.

# Chapter 2
# Beginning

What is Outreach? Its scope? Its potential? To whom or to what should Outreach efforts be first directed? How does one begin to develop this "thing" called Outreach which at first can seem to be so amorphous?

This chapter will address such basics. It will etch out for the reader tried and proven philosophy and approaches which can secure a foundation on which to build and organize effective social, health, and support programs for the parish's people. There are two essential positions the reader must be aware of prior to defining and projecting the parish's Outreach image.

**Welcome**

1. Critical to the development of an Outreach program, the Outreach director must convey to the people of the parish that all of them, especially those suffering, are welcome to call or visit the church and/or its rectory and offices. All must know that people who suffer will be welcomed in confidence, without judgment, without criticism, and without distinction. As soon as possible, parishioners should be made aware that anyone needing help can turn to the parish for help. Everyone must be invited to pray about and for people, especially the poor and the suffering. This prayerful, inviting approach will help to free people bound in silence. It will also create an immediate parish concern which will generate free-flowing ideas.

**Prayer**

2. Prayer is an essential ingredient to the development of Outreach as a parish based program. This becomes increasingly evident because:

(a) Prayer is strengthening and is needed when one cares

and serves people. Serving the neighbor can be challenging and sometimes difficult, even for Christians.

(b) Prayer is communication with God which motivates volunteers to remain faithful to the practice of Christ's compassion through serving the neighbor.

## Defining and Projecting the Parish's Outreach Image

The three immediate and easily available approaches which can be taken by the Outreach director and which lead to Outreach's definition and its beginning include speaking at the Sunday liturgies, utilizing the parish bulletin, and calling a general informational meeting.

1. *Speaking at the Sunday liturgies* allows the Outreach director the opportunity of quickly and directly reaching the majority of the parish's churchgoers. The talk should be based on the scriptural passages of that day. In the autumn the gospel cycle focuses on the miracles of Jesus. The epistle readings have to do with charitable works. These readings, coupled with the "new year" of a parish generally beginning in September, make this an ideal time for introducing an Outreach program to a parish.

When developing the material it is helpful to keep it loosely structured and for the director to keep himself or herself low-key. In other words, ask the people for help in discovering the needy through prayer and reflection. Ask them also to consider ways they might want to reach out with compassion to the suffering without criticism or distinction.

To assist the reader in developing your own ideas, a sample talk is included at the end of this chapter as a guide. The example given is based on James 2:1-5 which addresses attitudes toward the poor, and on Mark 7:31-37 where Jesus touches a deaf man and heals him in a sensitive and "private" way. To more fully appreciate the "strategy" of the sample talk, it is advisable to read and become familiar with the scriptural passages mentioned above.

2. *Utilizing the parish bulletin,* summarize what was said at the Sunday liturgy. This assures follow-up and provides the people at large with a clear and "tangible" idea of Outreach's framework. It would be wise that the Outreach director carve out a special and permanent place in the weekly bulletin for regular consciousness-raising blurbs and for sharing information about Outreach activity.

3. *Calling a general informational meeting* will put the Outreach director in direct contact with people and will enable him or her to "get a feel" for the people's responses to the bulletin blurbs and to the implied call of the introductory talk given at the Sunday liturgies. Parishioners should be invited to assist efforts to identify the general needs of the parish and the neighborhood. What vulnerabilities do they see? By way of the bulletin, advertise the meeting—for example,

> Outreach invites you to its first meeting. Come and see! A time for sharing ideas with no obligations. Wednesday, September 14 at 7:30 P.M. in the school hall.

Design the meeting in the context of a prayer service (see a sample service at the end of the chapter). After the opening hymn and prayer, read a passage used at the Sunday liturgy and speak about our faith and the Christian response to suffering. Include a recap of the talk given in the church. Outline the philosophy/theology of what is envisioned for Outreach, namely, the good Samaritan gospel story. After a responsorial psalm, the meeting agenda can be addressed. Ask the people to identify themselves by name and to express their reason for coming. Most likely the majority of people will say that they only came to see what was going to happen at this meeting. These people will remain relatively silent, but most likely will be attentive listeners for the duration of the meeting.

The overall perception of the vocal minority will probably indicate that the parish needs help, perhaps with the frail and elderly homebound. Others will be unsure of what other needs exist in the community. At the end of the discussion, invite any who wish to be available to Outreach to complete an "Interest Form" (see end of chapter). This tool is simple and designed to get an idea of where people feel comfortable/called to give time and energy should the need on the form develop into programs through Outreach. Remind them that at the time of this meeting there exist no organized means of serving the neighbor. Community needs still have to be determined. The "areas of interest" section on the interest form, therefore, is simply a guide for the director to use in determining (a) where people's interests for others might be, and (b) how much time people might like to devote to their "area of interest."

Once completed, the forms are collected. The meeting ends

with the continuation and termination of the prayer service, name-ly the Lord's Prayer and a closing spontaneous prayer of thanks.

It is to be noted that an occasional informational general meeting can become the forum of a feeling response leading to further volunteerism/action.

---

### SAMPLE TALK TO BEGIN OUTREACH PROGRAM

Today's reading warns us against judging by having two different standards in our minds. This letter of James challenges us to look into ourselves as Christians and to ask, "Do I let non-essentials get in the way of my being gracious, courteous, or loving toward another? Do I make room for those well dressed and wearing rings while I overlook or feel disgust for the person wearing shabby clothes? "My brothers and sisters," says St. James, "do not try to combine faith in Jesus Christ with the making of distinctions between classes of people."

Jesus himself was able to go beyond appearances. There was no criticism in him. Rather, Jesus saw and responded to the heart and the hurt within the human person. Jesus made room for the social rejects of his time. He washed lepers clean. He gave the woman caught in adultery another chance. He had compassion on the possessed and cast out their devils. He empathized with the lowly, and he raised the widow's dead son to life. He healed the sick who were brought to him, and in today's gospel he opened the ears of the deaf man and he restored his speech by putting his fingers into the man's ears and by touching his tongue with spittle.

How did Jesus come by the sensitivity of taking this deaf man aside and away from the crowd before healing him? What were the qualities in Jesus that gave him the courage to reach out and to physically touch others in their poverty and their want?

Jesus' strength was his love relationship to his Father. St. Luke tells us that oftentimes Jesus would teach in the temple by day and leave the city to spend the night on the Mount of Olives, and then at daybreak he went back to work. He spent the night on the Mount of Olives in prayer. Jesus prayed.

It was Jesus' intimate relationship to God, his Father, that gave clarity to Jesus' sensi-tive, one-standard vision—to know that it is the poor according to the world that God chooses to be rich in faith and to be the heirs of the kingdom.

As followers of Jesus, we too are to pray to the Father so that we may have the understanding, the sensitivity, and the courage to reach out to others regardless of their appearance, rich or poor.

Parish Outreach is us asking the Father to lead us to those in need because we want to reach out without class distinction to the suffering. Parish Outreach is an open-arm, open-heart attitude of looking into the heart and the hurt within the human person. Parish Outreach is making room for the social rejects of our time, to wash clean the AIDS victim, to assist a distraught woman to maintain her pregnancy, to have compassion for the mentally hurt, to understand the addicted, to listen to the bereaved, to minister to the homebound, to read for the blind, to shop for the elderly.

Parish Outreach is developing that loving, intimate prayer relationship with the Father that will give us the Jesus quality and the courage to reach out to the needy without making distinctions.

As the Outreach director at our parish, I joined the efforts you have already begun to build community through prayer, reflection and action. I am here to help you with the aid of God to continue to develop social, health and spiritual ministries which will reach into the homes and hearts of our parish community.

As I offer to help you help others, I ask you to help me to come to know and to sensitively understand the people and the concerns of our parish family.

Do you know a sick person who needs to be visited? Or a person grieving over the loss of a loved one? You can call the rectory. Do you know a family in which there is alcoholism or drug dependence? Or is there someone struggling to raise a child alone? Someone who needs financial assistance, or food, or a home? You can call or visit me at the rectory.

Do you yourself feel called to actively assist our parish's Outreach efforts? Contact me at the rectory. We are interested in you and you and you because Parish Outreach wants to reach out and influence for good as Jesus did without criticism. "By this will all know that you are my disciples, if you have love for one another."

OUTREACH
SAMPLE PRAYER SERVICE


HYMN


OPENING PRAYER    O God, we come together and ask your blessing. Send your Spirit upon us to help us to be patient, merciful and kind to all. May this Spirit of truth teach us the ways of Christ so that we may become gentle and compassionate to all people, especially the "needy neighbor" living in our own parish and community. Lead us to them in the name of Christ our Lord. Amen.


READING    The Parable of the Good Samaritan (Lk 10:25-37)
Following the reading there will be a *time for reflecting:*
- what must I do to receive eternal life?
- love of God
- love of neighbor
- a priest walked on by
- a Samaritan was filled with pity
- "Take care of him"
- *"Go then and do the same"*


PSALM RESPONSE    Psalm 62 (listening)


BUSINESS


CLOSING PRAYER    All loving God, strengthen us in our faith. Come into us and enable us to wholeheartedly serve our neighbor with compassion. We ask this through Christ our model. Amen.

# OUTREACH
## SAMPLE INTEREST FORM

Name: _____  Birthdate: _____
                                                                    Month/Day/Year
Address: _____  Home Phone: _____

_____  Business Phone: _____

Language(s) Spoken: _____

*AREA(S) OF INTEREST*

____ Retarded
____ Elderly-homebound
        ____ friendly visiting
        ____ personal care
        ____ housekeeping/laundry
        ____ transportation
        ____ shopping
        ____ supervision
        ____ other _____
____ Helping to meet people's basic needs
        ____ food
        ____ clothing
        ____ shelter
        ____ assist with application for Medicaid or food stamps
____ Assisting people who have mental or emotional problems
____ Helping people who are grieving over the loss of a
        ____ spouse
        ____ child
        ____ other _____
____ Spending time with a divorced or separated person
____ Helping Hispanic or other immigrants adjust to our neighborhood

### TIME AVAILABLE

| Day(s) Available | (Morning) | (Evening) |
|---|---|---|
| Monday | _____ | _____ |
| Tuesday | _____ | _____ |
| Wednesday | _____ | _____ |
| Thursday | _____ | _____ |
| Friday | _____ | _____ |
| Saturday | _____ | _____ |
| Sunday | _____ | _____ |

*PLEASE SHARE* one or more reasons which motivated you to offer to reach out to others through our parish's Outreach program (*use reverse side*). Thank you.

# Chapter 3
# The Bereavement Program

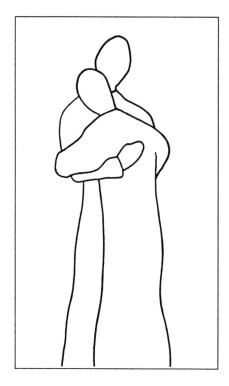

*Most loving God, you are mystery and God of consolation. You brought your only Son, Jesus, through suffering and death to a new and resurrected life. Use us, O God, to look with compassion upon those who mourn the death of loved ones. Give us the courage and the wisdom to sensitively share their pain and loss. Deepen our own faith so that we may confidently proclaim your promise of resurrection to all who mourn. Show your face to those who have died believing in the heavenly celebration promised by Jesus who is our hope and salvation. Amen.*

The bereavement program described herein aims to concretely and sensitively heal grieving people. It compassionately conveys to them Christian hope and genuine care. This program encourages individual attention by weaving together Outreach volunteers and grieving persons and families. Thus it promotes any needed healing between the sorrowing and/or the alienated and the local parish.

Any ethnically varied parish calls for a bereavement approach that has "universal sensitivity." The space and time needs of people in sorrow vary according to the culture and tradition of family and the personal needs of individuals within these families. Parish Outreach needs to develop a personalized bereavement program that will provide support and caring and that will be respectful of every person's right and need to mourn. Such a program waits on the readiness and willingness of a grieving person to receive the concern and the care of others. Initial contact by mail gives Outreach access to the sorrowing family without the possibility of unwittingly interfering, interrupting, or alienating their style or manner of grieving. Toward this end, four uniquely designed contacts are made by mail through Outreach volunteers. These mailings intend to progressively convey:

- the church community's sympathy and warmth;
- the parish's openness and readiness to be totally and personally available to the grieving at their convenience;
- the ongoing desire to support and care for them in their grief;
- the concrete demonstration of the Christian community's desire to reach out, draw in, and spiritually uplift sorrowing people by an annual liturgical opportunity followed by a gathering.

## Cards

*Card # 1*

The people and staff of
Our Lady of Lourdes Church
continue to pray for the Eternal Happiness of

_____

May the Risen Lord be the Comfort and Hope
of the Family.

_____                    _____
Pastor                                    Outreach Director

*Outside*                                         *Inside*

Card # 1 is simple in its design and message. Its approach is pastoral and tells the grieving family/person that all people continue to remember their loved one in prayer. The family receives this card within the month of the death of their beloved.

*Card #2*

Believe that_____

                              shares the fullness

                                        of God's Life.

Sincerely,

_____

Pastor, Our Lady of Lourdes Church

_____

Outreach Director

*Outside*                                    *Inside*

Card # 2 is a reminder to the family that their loved one lives fully with God. With this second contact, the family receives an invitation (see below) to call our Outreach program for assistance with their grief. The parish's openness and readiness is expressed by this little calling card:

*Sample calling card*

92-96 220th Street
Queens Village, New York 11428

*OUR LADY OF LOURDES
BEREAVEMENT PROGRAM*

Our Volunteers invite you to call us
for the assistance you may need
Call Outreach Phone # (718)479-5111

*Outside*

First Anniversary Prayers
continue for the
Eternal Happiness
of

_____

May the Risen Lord sustain you.

_____
Pastor, Our Lady of Lourdes Church

_____
Outreach Director

*Inside*

Card # 3 is "A First Anniversary Card." Like the other cards, this one reaches all families. The message of these anniversary prayers is that the beloved continues to live on eternally and in memory. This card evokes a most powerful response from grieving families who indicate that few, if any, people recall this meaningful event in their lives. It is a true sign of hope and love as this following letter testifies:

Dear Father and Sister,
I received the beautiful anniversary card last week and I want to thank you so much.
The card meant so much to me and my family. I have been going through a turmoil since my husband's death. Receiving the card at this particular time was an answer from heaven. Thank you again.

Sincerely,
Jane Doe

The People and Staff of
Our Lady of Lourdes Church
continue to pray for the Eternal Happiness of

_____

We invite you and your family to join us for a
Memorial Mass in the Church
on the Feast of All Saints
Sunday, November 1
at 5:00 p.m.

*Outside*                    *Inside*

Card # 4 is a joyful invitation to each person/family, encouraging them to invite others to join the people and the staff of the parish in commemorating and praying for the beloved by name at a liturgy. This invitation draws families and friends together at a liturgy specifically designed to support and uplift all who have lost a loved one over the past year. It is an opportunity for everyone to express grief as a Christian community, to find comfort, and to express belief in everlasting life. Following the liturgy, there is an opportunity for gathering together as a homogeneous group of people. Providing a time and place for sharing common feelings and responses to loss can further strengthen and heal.

## Volunteers

Intending to at least raise interest and questions among parishioners about the bereavement program, draft a bulletin blurb which is pastoral, clear, and inviting. Explain the importance of timeliness for people who mourn. Expose the volunteer role as non-threatening, simple and requiring a minimal time commitment. A sample bulletin blurb follows:

## Bereavement Volunteers Needed

Loss is always painful. This is especially so when families experience the ultimate loss—the death of someone they love. Mourning is a time of pain and of growth. It can be a time for God. Our parish is conscious that because each person is unique, people will grieve differently and according to their own personality, their culture and their family traditions. Our bereavement program wants to be sensitive and respectful to individual and family needs after the death of a loved one. Outreach to the bereaved seeks to reach people where they are at. God cares. We care. Through this program, volunteers offer people the consolation of the good news—that through the death and resurrection of Jesus, life is changed and not taken away. The bereavement program is about to begin. Through Outreach mailings, volunteers will initially convey our parish family caring and support during the time of loss. Each family will receive word from us by mail, and each year these families will receive a special invitation to participate in a eucharistic celebration honoring their deceased loved ones. Outreach encourages anyone willing to make mail contacts to please call Outreach for further information with no obligation.

Encourage a face-to-face contact with each respondent in order to better explain the program and to ascertain the needs, goals, and desires of the potential volunteer. Show each person the battery of cards and the simple mailing method to convey support to the grieving. This non-threatening personal encounter and the program's simple methods will put most volunteer anxieties to rest so that the bereavement program will have a smooth and comfortable beginning.

Method and volunteers in place, one must next discover who the deceased are and how to contact their nearest living relative or significant other. This can be an easy task as all parishes record such information in a log book. From such a parish register, a simple Outreach form can be designed to include the name of the deceased, the date of death, the name of the nearest relative, address, etc. (see sample Master Listing at the end of the chapter). All support mailing flows from this form to the grieving family.

Draw up a master list for each month. Assign a volunteer to do the mailings for one month's master list. Giving this volunteer the bereavement form for one month will require him or her to complete the four mailings to each family per year. For example, an immediate mailing is made to each family indicated by the bereavement form. Then six months later it is the same volunteer who is responsible for mailing card #2 to the same population. This is followed by the anniversary card (card #3) in six more months. Finally, each year in November, these same families receive card #4 inviting them to the memorial Mass and gathering. In this fashion, each volunteer is assigned one month of the year involving four mailings.

Meanwhile, after initiating the mailing, begin monthly meetings with all the bereavement volunteers. During these times, pray for the deceased and for their survivors to whom the parish's bereavement program ministers. This is also a time for deep discussion among volunteers about their own feelings concerning death, and their own belief in God and in an after-life. Speakers can be invited to address the needs of the grieving and how volunteers can best serve them. These meetings are an excellent and necessary preparation for volunteers who feel themselves ready and who wish to respond with a face to face contact with the grieving who call Outreach for personal assistance. Subsequent meetings of volunteers involve sharing from the volunteers who have had personal contact with grieving people. This evokes a problem solving agenda and the natural education of all volunteers. The meetings should be lively, joyful, albeit sometimes bittersweet, and always deeply spiritual and meaningful.

# OUTREACH
## BEREAVEMENT MINISTRY
### *Master Listing*

| Name | Registration Number | Age | Name of Nearest Relative | Address | Date of Death | Funeral Director |
|------|---------------------|-----|--------------------------|---------|---------------|------------------|
|      |                     |     |                          |         |               |                  |
|      |                     |     |                          |         |               |                  |
|      |                     |     |                          |         |               |                  |
|      |                     |     |                          |         |               |                  |
|      |                     |     |                          |         |               |                  |
|      |                     |     |                          |         |               |                  |
|      |                     |     |                          |         |               |                  |
|      |                     |     |                          |         |               |                  |
|      |                     |     |                          |         |               |                  |
|      |                     |     |                          |         |               |                  |
|      |                     |     |                          |         |               |                  |
|      |                     |     |                          |         |               |                  |
|      |                     |     |                          |         |               |                  |
|      |                     |     |                          |         |               |                  |

# Chapter 4
# Flower Ministry Program

*O God, you are the author and lover of peace, the source of all holy desires. To know you is to live; to serve you is to reign. Through the intercession of Mary, the queen of peace, grant us, O God, that peace which the world cannot give, so that we may enjoy peace in our days and freedom from the fear of any evil. We ask this of you in Jesus' name and through your Holy Spirit.*

*Hail, Mary, Queen of Peace, Pray For Us!*

The simple program goal of a flower ministry program is "to bring sunshine and hope into parish homes and hearts by having neighborhood youth deliver flowers to the sick, the disabled, and the lonely."

To initiate such a program, the Outreach director should meet with the director of the local funeral parlor to tell him of the goal of the parish's flower ministry program and of its potential of bringing positive things to the neighborhood. Besides bringing sunshine and hope into the homes, it would encourage goodness in the neighborhood youth. Evoke from the funeral director his own thoughts concerning the possible desire on the part of the families of the deceased to donate the leftover or left-behind flowers from the wakes of their beloved dead. The Outreach director may learn that many flowers are wasted since they cannot be brought to the cemetery, and that families often verbalize their sorrow and frustration at having to discard these beautiful flowers.

A formal and sensitive written request, or "invitation" from the church is a gentle way of informing potential donors. Here is a sample invitation:

---

*THE INVITATION*

Flowers can be donated in memory of your beloved deceased to Our Lady of Lourdes Outreach Program. Donated flowers will be appropriately prepared and delivered to the sick and disabled of the parish by neighborhood youth. Your gift of flowers will bring sunshine and hope into homes and hearts.
Thank you.

*AND THE ENVELOPE*

Our Lady of Lourdes Outreach
Flower Ministry Program

---

This invitation is distributed by the funeral director to each grieving family at the time when the family is receiving other written materials for confirming funeral arrangements. The funeral director also completes a flower ministry form for all flower donors:

---

FLOWER MINISTRY FORM

Date: _____

Name of Deceased: _____

Name of Person Donating Flowers: _____

Address:_____

Relationship to Deceased: _____

Signature of Person Donating Flowers: _____

Thank You!

---

The flower ministry form initiates a letter of thanks from Outreach to all donors:

---

**SAMPLE LETTER OF THANKS**

Dear (Name of Donor),

Our Lady of Lourdes flower ministry program accepts with sincere appreciation the flowers donated in memory of (name of deceased).

May these special flowers bring peace and joy to the sick of our parish and God's comfort to you and your family.

Respectfully and gratefully,

_____

Outreach Director

---

Assured of the cooperation between funeral parlor personnel and Outreach, the director of Outreach then approaches the manager of a nearby florist. Once again the idea of a flower ministry program needs to be explained in detail to the florist owner or manager. Indicate that an enthusiastic and concrete response has already been procured from the funeral director and that the church, after using the donated flowers, would like to return all flower stands and vases to the florist. If the owner seems interested in the project, his cooperation is solicited, and he can be directly asked to assist the program with a supply of florist paper which will be used to wrap the flowers into floral bouquets to be delivered to the people. Flowers and paper forthcoming, it is now necessary to target the population who will receive these flowers and develop an orderly method (procedure) to distribute the flowers.

## Targeting

Targeting the population "sick, disabled, lonely" is usually easy. The parish priest's visitation list to selected ill and homebound people is an excellent beginning.

Parish records and other Outreach programs can suggest other needy people in the neighborhood. These include:

- bereavement program names;
- rectory log books of relatives of the recently deceased;
- people in the homebound program;
- names from recent anointings.

Make a file box of all these people who meet the criteria to receive the donated flowers. Record each person on a file card, including name, address, and telephone number and other information which would be helpful for fine-tuning the approach for delivering flowers.

An example is given below:

---

### THE CARD: FOR COORDINATOR USE

Name: _____

Address: _____

Telephone: _____

In Memory of: _____ Date: _____

Delivery Date: _____ Delivered By: _____

---

"In memory of" refers to those people selected to receive flowers from the church's records of the recently deceased. When flowers are delivered to their living relative, it is sensitive and pastoral to inform the receiver that through these flowers delivered to them, their beloved deceased will continue to be remembered by parishioners in prayer.

Also indicated on the card is the date that flowers are sent to a particular home as well as the name of the youth who delivered the flowers.

To assure that the volunteer youth deliverer receives his or her assignment, and knows to whom and where to deliver the flowers, a second card, similar but not exactly the same as the first, is essential. To be quickly identifiable, this second card should be colored. It includes the name and address of the person to receive the flowers and a place for the signature of the person accepting the flowers. This colored card is ultimately returned to the church's Outreach office as confirmation that the flowers were indeed delivered by the youth and received by the targeted person/family. A sample of this colored card is given below.

```
┌─────────────────────────────────────────────────────────────┐
│              THE CARD: FOR USE BY VOLUNTEER TEEN              │
│                                                               │
│                    Delivery date: _____   │
│                                                               │
│   Name: _____  │
│                                                               │
│   Address:_____   │
│                                                               │
│   Delivered by:_____   │
│                                                               │
│   Signature of receiver: _____   │
│                                                               │
│                                                               │
└─────────────────────────────────────────────────────────────┘
```

Both sets of cards are maintained in the file box of people targeted to receive flowers. The use and usefulness of the cards will be explained after all program elements are set in place. Volunteers are the final ingredient needed to activate a flower ministry program.


## Recruiting Volunteers: Adults

The "ideal" would be to have a few coordinating adults and a cadre of young people (teens) to do the footwork of delivering. Adults are needed to pick up the flowers from the funeral parlor. Adult volunteers, therefore, would need a car and they would have to be willing to put up with loose flower petals falling on the inside of their vehicles. Ideally these volunteers take the flowers to their own homes where they separate the good from the "used" flowers, wrapping the good ones and preparing them for delivery.

In recruiting the adult volunteers for the flower ministry program, use the parish bulletin. Explain the overall goals of the program and the enthusiasm of the "nearby businesses." Without giving all the details of projected hopes, simply invite any person interested in making floral bouquets to call the rectory office. These volunteers are interviewed, as is each volunteer in all Outreach programs. The adult volunteers are called "flower ministry coordinators."

## Recruiting Volunteers: Teens

Strategies are needed:

1. to attract highly motivated youths to serve their neighbors through a flower ministry program;
2. to ensure parental consent and support for young people in ministry who will be walking the neighborhood delivering flowers.

Various approaches can be used simultaneously or independently according to the design and the desired rate of development of the parish's flower ministry program. Some suggestions follow:

- When soliciting the young (non-adult) volunteers, refer to them as "teens" and "flower ministers."

- Utilize a flower ministry application (see sample below) to

---

### FLOWER MINISTRY APPLICATION

Today's Date _____

Name _____     Birthdate _____

Address _____     Phone Number _____

School _____     Grade _____

Teacher _____

I want to be a flower minister because:

_____

_____

_____

_____

_____

_____

_____

_____

_____

Signature of parent _____

---

include basic volunteer information, school attended, grade and teacher. Most importantly of all, flower ministry applications should have plenty of room for the youth to explain in his or her own words the motivation for the volunteering. This, plus the parent signature at the bottom, is the "go" sign for acceptance of the applicant.

- Use the parish bulletin

---

### PARISH BULLETIN ANNOUNCEMENT

Our parish is planning a flower ministry program which will provide grieving, lonely, homebound persons with a cheerful message of a bouquet of flowers and a promise of prayerful remembrance. Our flower ministry program needs people to deliver flowers. Our ministers must be teens who have been confirmed (or who are preparing for the sacrament of confirmation) and who desire to bring good wishes and flowers to those in need. Following the example of Jesus, flower ministers care about others. Flower ministers give time and energy to help others feel happier. By being good people themselves, flower ministers give positive example to their peers. Flower ministers improve the reputation of teenagers in and around the neighborhood area by their consistently excellent behavior. Here's how it works: The teenage flower minister will pick up the prepared flowers and a card from the flower ministry coordinator's house. He or she will deliver flowers to the home designated by the coordinator and listed on the card. At the time of delivery, the card will be signed at the door by the person receiving the flowers. Finally, the signed card will be brought to the Outreach office by the flower minister.

If you are interested in becoming a flower minister, please stop by the Outreach office to pick up an application.

---

- Leave some applications at the doors of the church and school.

- Give applications to all confirmation age students in the parish school and religious education program.

Once selected, each applicant (now volunteer) receives a personal letter (see sample on next page) from the director to formally activate him or her as a flower minister. Besides giving a starting point to the young volunteer, this letter eases the minds of the parents who might be concerned about whose home their child is expected to visit to pick up the flowers.

SAMPLE PERSONAL LETTER

Dear Flower Minister:

Thank you so much for joining Our Lady of Lourdes Flower Ministry Program!

Soon you will receive your first phone call from _____ , the flower ministry coordinator. You will be asked to go to the coordinator's home

Name of Flower Minister Coordinator

Address

Telephone Number

to pick up a bouquet of flowers. These flowers are to be delivered to someone in the neighborhood. You do not have to enter the house where the flowers are delivered. Simply ring the bell and hand the flowers to the person who answers the door. There will be an orange card for the person to sign at the door. That's all! You have done a beautiful thing for God!

Please remember to return all orange cards to the Outreach office. (You can put them through the mail slot in the rectory door.)

I thank you again, and your family too, for supporting this good work.

Good luck, and God be with you!

Sincerely in Christ,

Name of Outreach Director

With the following in place:
- donated flowers and paper
- invitations to donate flowers
- the population targeted to receive the flowers
- the volunteers—adult and youth,

a kick-off meeting with adult volunteers is suggested. Here roles are clearly defined, schedules are put in place, and a system is rehearsed.

**The Kickoff**

Begin the meeting with a prayer, followed by time for discussion and informal sharing. Finally, give each of the adult volunteers (flower ministry coordinators):

(1) A schedule indicating the day of their two hours of volunteerism (see below). Decide, for example, that on

Monday and Thursday volunteer #1 will pick up and prepare the flowers. On Tuesday and Friday, it will be the job of volunteer #2, etc. (The schedule below is based on four adult volunteers and can be easily adjusted to accommodate a lesser or a greater number of volunteer coordinators.)

| | |
|---|---|
| Monday | Volunteer #1 |
| Tuesday | Volunteer #2 |
| Wednesday | Volunteer #3 |
| Thursday | Volunteer #1 |
| Friday | Volunteer #2 |
| Saturday | Volunteer #4 |
| Sunday | No Flowers |

It should be noted that the time limitation of each volunteer is respected by the schedule. Volunteers #3 and #4, according to the sample, are utilized one day, whereas the other two volunteer two days a week. *Also of note is that the work involved in flower ministry does not take the entire day.* For example, flowers can be picked up from the funeral parlor by the flower ministry coordinator at 4:00 P.M. and the entire work can be accomplished by 6:00 P.M. While the schedule indicates days, *we are really talking about volunteering for approximately one to two hours per "day."*

(2) A list of flower ministers/youth volunteers (see sample volunteer form, page 37).

(3) A file box containing the white cards and the colored cards indicating the people targeted to receive the flowers.

(4) A prayer card (on the back of which is the name and address of the parish) to be stapled on each prepared bouquet (sample prayer is at the beginning of this chapter).

(5) An outline and review of the procedure to be followed by the Outreach volunteers (see sample procedure form, page 39).

Explain and discuss the schedule, procedure, and general expectations of the flower ministry program. Fielding questions and encouraging feedback allows all coordinators to arrive at a level of comfort and readiness. The meeting can end with a short, spontaneous prayer.

Coordinator Name: _____

## OUTREACH: FLOWER MINISTRY YOUTH VOLUNTEERS

| Flower Minister Name | Grade | Birthday | Address & Phone | Delivery Dates | | | | | | Delivered to |
|---|---|---|---|---|---|---|---|---|---|---|
| | | | | | | | | | | |
| | | | | | | | | | | |
| | | | | | | | | | | |
| | | | | | | | | | | |
| | | | | | | | | | | |
| | | | | | | | | | | |
| | | | | | | | | | | |
| | | | | | | | | | | |

# OUTREACH: FLOWER MINISTRY PROCEDURE

| Outreach Director | Coordinator | Youth | Receiver |
|---|---|---|---|
| | 1. Phones funeral parlor to verify donated flowers. | | |
| | 2. Picks up flowers and forwards flower ministry form from funeral parlor to Outreach director. | | |
| 3. Initiates letter of thanks to all flower donors. | | | |
| | 4. Wraps flowers in florist paper. | | |
| | 5. Attaches prayer of peace to bouquet. | | |
| | 6. Uses information on file card to phone potential receiver. Informs person that flowers from Outreach are forthcoming. | | |
| | 7. Alerts teen that there are flowers to be delivered. | | |
| | | 8. Receives orange card. Delivers flowers to receiver. | |
| | | | 9. Receives flowers and signs orange card. |
| | | 10. Returns orange card to Outreach office. | |
| 11. Files orange card. | | | |

# Chapter 5
# The Homebound Program

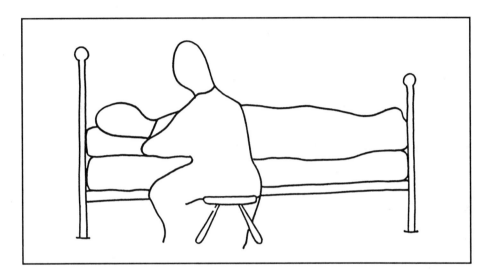

*All-powerful and ever-living God, the lasting health of all who believe in you, hear us as we ask your loving help for _____. Send your Spirit upon him/her so that he/she may be strengthened to realize that he/she is joined to Christ through the suffering and pain he/she suffers. Heal and guide _____ every moment of his/her life. Through this prayer and our good works we wish to unite ourselves to you, Father, and we ask that this prayer be accepted and answered by you in and through Jesus Christ our Lord. Amen.*

A parish's homebound program aims to assist people who reside in the parish boundaries and who are made homebound through physical impairment, old age and/or certain debilitating symptomatology such as those caused by Alzheimer's disease, senility, fragility, AIDS and the like. Outreach's assistance to the elderly and sick through program creation can develop from an awareness already existent among the parish priests and eucharistic ministers who usually are acquainted with and spiritually minister to the parish's less mobile, ill, and elderly people.

Thus for the Outreach director, the parish's "sick call" or communion list becomes a helpful and immediate tool with which to become familiar. To such a list, add all incoming phone calls asking for home assistance. These contacts are usually made by the homebound persons or by their family and friends. Record the time, request, telephone number or an address for the caller as well as for the person in need (see Telephone Assessment Form, pages 55–56). Each person on the list (sick call/communion list and phone contacts) should receive a telephone call from the Outreach director who makes each one aware of Outreach's desire to pay them a friendly visit.

To avoid touching upon people's inner vulnerability or putting them in a dependent position and engendering resentment, make no mention of any future parish plans for a homebound program which might assist people in need.

Rather, the initial visit to homebound people is primarily a friendly open pastoral encounter where each party can come to know each other comfortably and without feelings of defensiveness. Meanwhile, for the Outreach director as a professional, many mental notes should be made concerning environmental safety, physical independence vs. dependence, social status, family support systems, and feelings of self-worth. Subtly guide the conversation to obtain an overall general psychosocial assessment.

Of course, as in any homebound situation, a variety of unmet needs will be discovered. Oftentimes the spiritual support provided by parish priests and eucharistic ministers is real, yet at the same time an Outreach visit will surface a tremendous amount of anxiety on the part of the family regarding the corporal needs of elderly and/or sick persons. Frequently there will not be agreement among the elderly person and the family member as to how much physical or emotional help the elderly person or family really needs. Through sometimes painful discussion, dialogue and counseling with the family, the director and all parties involved agree upon an acceptable plan of action on behalf of the elder person as well as families.

At the end of each encounter in the targeted homes it is helpful to ask these homebound persons if they know anyone else in the parish wanting such a visit. Such an approach will swell the Outreach visitation list as most homebound people are eager to share names of their area friends who are in need or who they believe would at least enjoy a visit from the parish.

People of God deserve the best that the church has to offer. It is possible to develop a qualitative and professional homebound program within a parish setting by beginning very simply.

An excellent initial tool for exciting, facilitating and enabling volunteers who will assist with visits to, and assistance in, the homes of the elderly and homebound is the parish bulletin. (See Chapter 8 on consciousness raising.)

Use the bulletin to ask for a nurse to help with home assessments and for non-nurse volunteers to help the elderly with simple needs. Remember to keep the blurbs short, get to the point quickly, and be conscious of the time constraints of potential volunteers. Examples follow:

---

*(1) The help of _one_ nurse:*
"Is there a nurse who can help me assess the needs of the elderly? Consider donating _one hour_ of your time each month."

*(2) "Lay" (non-nurse) assistance for shopping:*
"There is a small, frail, delicate woman in our parish who is 92 years old. She can no longer do her weekly shopping and is requesting someone to assist her. Is there someone in the parish who can do light shopping for this elderly woman?"

---

Simple direct requests evoke awareness with concomitant feelings. The response to such bulletin blurbs will be forthcoming and positive.

Respondents usually phone Outreach. They will not know that perhaps others will have also offered their services. Each caller needs to speak directly with the Outreach director who thanks them and invites them to come into the rectory for a discussion of the situation without any obligation to get further involved. Some volunteers will decline the invitation, saying that they don't want to be known and they don't want to commit themselves. While being firm on the necessity of face to face encounter, assure them that talk, not commitment, is the objective.

Most respondents, on the other hand, are glad for the offer to meet with the Outreach director, and they gladly come into the rectory as invited.

When visiting with the potential nurse volunteer, detail the professional approach aspired to by the newly developing homebound program. Indicate that a professional assessment of the elderly person, family and environment would help achieve such a professional program.

To clarify and facilitate the "job" of the nurse volunteer, show her simple assessment guides (see samples, pages 57–60) which will help clarify expectations. Place the name, address and phone number of each potential nurse volunteer on a volunteer information form (see sample, pages 61–62) and alphabetically file it in an Outreach volunteer log book. Use a divider to separate nurse volunteers from lay (non-nurse) volunteers.

A face to face discussion with the lay (non-nurse) potential volunteer takes on a human interest approach. It is the non-nurse volunteer who provides direct services to the homebound as warranted by individual circumstances and by the nurse's assessment. Volunteer services include shopping, cooking, personal care, feeding, laundry, housekeeping and companionship. All homebound volunteers are supported in their ministry by the professional nurse volunteer who orients them to the home and the family of the homebound, who answers their questions, and who initially acts as a role model in delivering quality and caring services.

Speak to the potential volunteer about the needs of the woman mentioned in the blurb, but without mentioning the woman's name. Most potential volunteers will evidence caring and compassion for the old woman. Some will be enthusiastic about shopping for the elderly person. It is then that each is told that the bulletin blurb evoked several respondents and that only one volunteer is needed to shop for this elderly person. Ask the potential volunteer: If there are other people in the parish in similar circumstances, would you still be willing to shop for someone? Most will agree. As with the potential nurse volunteer, so with the potential lay volunteer, alphabetically enter each volunteer shopper in the volunteer log book.

Having the service of nurse(s) for one hour each month allows the director additional hours of time to assist with incoming calls, write bulletin requests, interview volunteers, and select the person (lay/non-nurse volunteer) to assess the elderly. It is to the professional nurse(s) that credit goes for the quality of care received by homebound parishioners and for the comprehensive and holistic services rendered. All people accepted into the homebound program are visited by a professional nurse volunteer who helps the family assess the real needs of the homebound individual and his or her family. The nurse offers health counseling and care planning to the family in the home setting. As many family members as possible should be involved in their initial Outreach nurse volunteer visit which is intended to be therapeutic and helpful for the entire family.

As visits by the director and by the volunteer nurses to the elderly and their homebound friends continue, follow up with bulletin information (consciousness raising) and requests (calls for compassion), which become progressively challenging to potential volunteers. Gradually ask for people to help with specific and graduating needs: shopping, companionship, cooking, cleaning, bathing, and other personal care. Each blurb should be as personal and as simple as the sample given, and each should evoke numbers of responses.

Individually interview all respondents and log all information. Allow 3 to 6 months to accumulate enough volunteers for a formal program beginning.

The following pages detail for you, the reader, a procedural flow of people and papers which make a homebound program come alive. A couple of case studies highlighting the program's specific effect will follow.

*Example A: The Early Days*

The example below shows that the director is obviously the hub of the homebound activities. The input and advice of the assessment nurses is offered to the director who receives all information, controls all decision making and provides most of the service. The Early Days: Procedural Flow (Example A) is very simple.

---

EXAMPLE A
THE EARLY DAYS: PROCEDURAL FLOW

| *Director* | *Assessment Nurse* |
|---|---|
| (1) receives telephone call or office visit regarding need for assistance. | |
| (2) calls assessment nurse. | |
| | (3) does home assessment. |
| | (4) forwards assessment to director. |
| (5) receives home assessment, refers to the homebound volunteer book, and chooses appropriate volunteer. | |
| (6) meets with selected volunteer and takes her into the home of the elderly/sick. | |
| (7) makes monthly follow-up calls to Outreach volunteer and homebound recipient of care to ensure quality and caring service. | |

---

As the homebound program grows to involve literally hundreds of receivers of care and givers of compassion, decentralization becomes the name of the game for the director who has no

# EXAMPLE B

## LATER DEVELOPMENTS: PROCEDURAL FLOW

| Director | Nurse Coordinator | Assessment Nurse | Volunteer Coordinator | Follow-up Coordinator |
|---|---|---|---|---|
| (1) Receives Triage Form (see sample, p. 147) from phone volunteer.<br>(2) Refers Triage Form to nurse coordinator. | | | | |
| | (3) Makes professional telephone assessment.<br>(4) Relays above information and refers homebound to assessment nurse. | | | |
| | | 5) Makes Home Assessment (see pp. 57–60).<br>(6) Completes Home Assessment Form.<br>(7) Forwards Home Assessment Form to Outreach Office. | | |

- - - - - - - - - - - - - - (8) MATCH-MAKING MEETING - - - - - - - - - - - - - -

| Director | Nurse Coordinator | Assessment Nurse | Volunteer Coordinator | Follow-up Coordinator |
|---|---|---|---|---|
| | | | (9) Phones volunteer to discuss homebound need.<br>(10) Advises and refers volunteer to home assessment nurse.<br>(11) Introduces volunteer to homebound person/family.<br>(12) Instructs volunteer in care of homebound. | |
| (13) Acts as liaison and advocate for homebound with area agencies and providers to ensure comprehensive care and holistic approach. | | | | (14) Regularly phones volunteer and homebound family for "trouble-shooting" and health promotion. |

choice but to review and revamp the ratio of the care he or she provides versus the care he or she directs.

*Example B: Later Developments*

Example B (p. 46) builds upon the basic procedural flow shown in Example A. While Example A utilizes the expertise of a director and a nurse volunteer responsible for visiting homes and assessing people's real needs, Example B utilizes three volunteer leaders: the nurse coordinator, the volunteer (non-nurse) coordinator and the follow-up coordinator.

Each of these leaders under the direction of the Outreach director coordinates and supervises the activities of numerous volunteers.

In Example B, for instance, the director defers to a nurse coordinator who now assumes the role of direct contact with family members. It is this coordinator who contacts the caller and professionally records a telephone assessment by phone (see Telephone Assessment Form, pages 55–56) and then, based on her information and experience, the nurse coordinator peruses the homebound volunteer book and makes her choice of the assessment nurse. Note that it is the coordinator and not the director (as in Example A) who maintains all contact with the caller and/or family and who, with the assessment nurse, will make the home visit. As in Example A, so in Example B, the home assessment is completed by the assessment nurse. The nurse coordinator then reviews the home assessment with the assessment nurse and makes a presentation of the findings at the match-making meeting. The director chairs the match-making meeting which exists as a coordinating effort for the sharing of information among coordinators, the selection of the volunteer for the specific needs of the homebound, and any necessary problem solving.

The volunteer coordinator is the only non-nurse in a leadership position in Outreach's homebound program. It is the volunteer coordinator who hears the needs of the homebound person as presented by the nurse coordinator at the match-making meeting. The volunteer coordinator assisted by the director selects the lay volunteer most suited to address the needs of the homebound family. The director's assistance in selecting the homebound volunteer is advisable because it is the director who has the advantage of having had a lengthy interview and therefore presumably deeper knowledge of each homebound volunteer's likes, dislikes, talents and personality. Hence, the match made should be more personalized and successful in meeting the needs and satisfying both the homebound family and the homebound volunteer.

Match-making completed, it is the volunteer coordinator who describes the needs of the homebound person/family to the lay (non-nurse) volunteer in order to reassess his or her consent to volunteer. The volunteer coordinator then notifies the same home assessment nurse who made the initial assessment. The assessment nurse arranges with the volunteer to meet in the home of the family in order to flesh out and initiate the plan of care.

The follow-up coordinator's responsibility is to ensure a mutual comfort level and mutual satisfaction between the now active homebound volunteer and homebound family by contacting each. These telephone contacts become regular and monthly. They help certify consistent high quality caring and respect between the homebound volunteer and the person/family cared for. The follow-up coordinator as nurse can advise, comfort, and problem solve for both sides as needed and appropriate. Her input is valuable in the maintenance of the overall plan of care. She signals confidence and security and plays an important role in health promotion for family and homebound volunteer alike. Finally, Example B allows the director time to act as liaison and advocate with health providers and social service agencies where needed on behalf of the elderly and/or the elderly homebound family. The three case studies presented below will help to clarify the procedural flow of the Outreach homebound program.

The examples are also purposely selected to give the reader a feel for and a comfortableness with

  – the diversity of people who call the church for help in their home;
  – the broad range of necessities (from the simple to the complex) calling for Outreach attention;
  – the uniqueness and utilization of volunteers according to their interests, age and circumstances.

Anonymity: Names have been changed and some circumstances altered to preserve confidentiality. The stories are true.

## CASE #1

*THE CALL FOR HELP:*

Ms. Z is a seventy-eight year old woman living alone in a small apartment. Her niece called Outreach for help. Upon conversation with the nurse coordinator Outreach learned that Ms. Z had become forgetful and disoriented. Neighbors discovered her outside at all hours wandering the neighborhood and picking garbage. Ms. Z never married and has no family except her niece who has several small children and who lives more than thirty minutes away. Her niece thinks that her aunt needs to be in a nursing home. She doesn't know where to turn and is very concerned with her "deteriorating aunt."

*OUTREACH INTERVENTION:*

The nurse coordinator assigns Ms. Z to an Outreach volunteer nurse assessor who visits Ms. Z with the niece present. The nurse assessor uses the home assessment form (see sample, pages 59–60) and reports:

> "Ms. Z is a small, frail, pleasant, smiling little lady. She is very cooperative and can carry on a simple but distracted conversation. She is very anxious, picks at her clothes, and has tremors of her hands and sometimes her body. She cries frequently. Ms. Z can wash and toilet herself. She often forgets to eat and never touches the stove. Ms. Z's three-room apartment is neglected. Financially, Ms. Z has no savings and has been living on Social Security coupled with monthly financial assistance from her niece. The niece visits her aunt weekly, shops for her and helps with the vacuuming and dusting."

The assessment nurse further suggests:
- Perhaps Ms. Z could profit from medical intervention.
- Ms. Z may be eligible for Medicaid.
- Ms. Z would benefit from a minimum of eight hours of assistance at home.
- Ms. Z is unable to attend church and expressed the desire for prayer at home.

The match-making meeting follows where the Outreach homebound coordinators review and discuss the assessment nurse's findings concerning Ms. Z. It is at this match-making meeting where planning for Ms. Z converts into prayer, problem solving, and action on her behalf.

The director as liaison and advocate:
- contacted Ms. Z's doctor and an anti-anxiety medication was ordered.
- counseled Ms. Z's niece and mailed a Medicaid application to Ms. Z's home for completion by the niece.
- referred Ms. Z to the parish priest and eucharistic ministers for regular pastoral and sacramental visits.

The volunteer (non-nurse) coordinator:
- assisted by the director selected the volunteer most suited to daily (9 to 5) bathe, cook, shop, do housekeeping and laundry for Ms. Z.

– contacted the assessment nurse who escorted and introduced the selected Outreach volunteer to Ms. Z and her niece.

The follow-up coordinator made a note to call Ms. Z's niece as well as the Outreach volunteer assisting her aunt during the first week of the Outreach home assistance and each third week thereafter. Over time the follow-up coordinator regularly evaluates the overall program implementation for Ms. Z.

*EVALUATION:*

The follow-up coordinator's report told us that "Ms. Z's anxiety was greatly relieved by the prescribed medication and by the daily presence of the Outreach volunteer. Her tremors ceased and she no longer picked at her clothing. She appeared more relaxed, didn't cry, and her conversations were more coherent. She appreciated praying with the parish eucharistic ministers and receiving the eucharist weekly. Ms. Z's appetite was excellent. She ate three balanced meals each day. The niece became increasingly comfortable with the homebound volunteer. She was greatly relieved knowing that her aunt's basic needs for safety, care, and emotional and spiritual support were being met. The apartment was painted by the landlord and kept up by the volunteer. Medicaid was acquired which then entitled Ms. Z to twenty-four hours' live-in services. The homebound volunteer accepted this position which saved Ms. Z from having to adjust to a new face. It also provided employment and income to the homebound volunteer. The niece no longer had to supplement her aunt's Social Security.

Six months after Outreach intervention Ms. Z appeared as a well-cared-for, gentle little lady. She was calm and enjoyed going for walks with the homebound volunteer. Ms. Z's niece said that the volunteer is like a sister to her aunt, and the niece is very grateful. The niece put aside nursing home consideration for Ms. Z because her aunt was safely and satisfactorily maintained at home.

# CASE #2

*THE CALL FOR HELP:*
A neighbor anonymously informed Outreach about Mr. Q who was reported to be forty years old, suffering from a terminal illness and living alone.

*OUTREACH INTERVENTION:*
The nurse coordinator received this cry for help on Mr. Q's behalf but was unable to glean a telephone assessment because of Mr. Q's hesitancy over the phone. However, Mr. Q was amenable to a visit "from the parish." A volunteer assessment nurse was assigned by the nurse coordinator to assess Mr. Q and his overall situation. The home assessment revealed Mr. Q to be a gentle professional man in his forties. Upon learning of his illness one year prior to the call to Outreach, Mr. Q resigned as a high school science teacher. Because of medical expenses Mr. Q exhausted his savings and is embarrassed and silent about having to live like a poor man. He keeps his apartment spotless in spite of his pain and physical disability. He eats inadequately because his appetite is poor. Mr. Q has little money for food, and often the shopping and the weight of the packages are too much for him. He says he never applied for financial assistance because he is too ill and he certainly would not be able to spend any length of time in any waiting area.

The assessment nurse "connected" with this very pale, underweight, weak and short of breath man who confided in her his many years of being in the third order of a religious congregation. He shed tears over his inability to walk to or to assist at church services. He shared pictures of his own religious art work with the assessment nurse who offered him the hope of praying and receiving the sacraments in his own home. The assessment nurse reported these findings to the nurse coordinator for presentation at the match-making meeting, and the director made an immediate referral to:
  • the parish priest for Mr. Q's receptivity to prayer, the sacrament of reconciliation, eucharist and the sacrament of the sick;
  • the Saint Vincent de Paul Society for prayerful visits;
  • the city's human service agency for immediate financial and medical assistance for Mr. Q at home;
  • the parish's Outreach food program which delivered food to his home on a weekly basis.

The volunteer coordinator:
  • selected an Outreach volunteer to assist Mr. Q with cooking and housekeeping twice weekly.
  • contacted the assessment nurse who escorted the homebound volunteer into Mr. Q's home for introductions and to initiate care.

The follow-up coordinator continued regular telephone contact with Mr. Q and with the volunteer to ensure quality care and mutual satisfaction.

*EVALUATION:*

Mr. Q was very content with the services of Outreach. He became emotionally comfortable enough to continue to utilize Outreach for ongoing support and encouragement. As his illness progressed Outreach services to him increased. Four months before his death, Mr. Q's only relative, a brother, had Mr. Q transferred by ambulance to his own home out of state. Upon Mr. Q's death his brother expressed gratitude to Outreach for the loving, prayerful attention his brother had received from the parish Outreach program.

## CASE #3

*THE CALL FOR HELP:*
Mrs. B is a seventy-five year old woman living alone in a private home. She called for help, citing that her children and grandchildren live at a distance and she feels unable to cope with the outdoor home management.

*INTERVENTION:*
The nurse coordinator by phone learned that Mrs. B has a chronic illness and walks with the assistance of a cane. She manages her own shopping and cooking. She keeps up the house and wants to retain as much independence as possible. But in the winter, Mrs. B frets because of the snow; in the fall, it is the leaves; and in the spring and the summer, well—the grass grows and so do the weeds. She is financially secure. After referral by the nurse coordinator, the assessment nurse visited Mrs. B at home. The home assessment was in complete accord with the nurse coordinator's telephone assessment. At the match-making meeting the volunteer coordinator selected a teenage volunteer to assist Mrs. B with seasonal outdoor work. Introductions between the teen and Mrs. B were conducted in Mrs. B's home by the assessment nurse.

*EVALUATION:*
Follow-up by phone revealed the ongoing satisfaction and meeting of expectations by Mrs. B and her teenage Outreach volunteer.

# OUTREACH
## HOMEBOUND PROGRAM
*Telephone Assessment Form*

Name _____ Date _____ Age _____

Address _____ Apt. #_____

Telephone _____ Language_____

---

Referred by _____ Relationship _____

Telephone _____

---

*Activity*                          *Aids*
____ ambulatory      ____ lives alone      ____ cane        ____ catheter
____ non-ambulatory  ____ with spouse      ____ wheelchair  ____ dentures
____ homebound       ____ with children    ____ walker      ____ prosthesis
____ non-homebound   ____ other            ____ bedpan

---

Nearest Contact Person_____ Relationship _____

Telephone _____

---

*Limitations:*
____ stroke       ____ diabetes     ____ visual impairment
____ heart        ____ cancer       ____ hearing impairment
____ arthritis    ____ speech       ____ paralysis

_____
_____

*Mental Status:*
____ alert      ____ agitated/restless    ____ confused     ____ depressed    ____ hostile

_____
_____
_____
_____

Assessed by: _____

# OUTREACH
# HOMEBOUND PROGRAM
## *Home Assessment Checklist*

Name _____ Age _____ Date _____

Address _____ Apt. #_____

_____ Telephone _____

---

In case of emergency, contact_____

Relationship _____ Telephone _____

---

*Physical Description (weight):*
____ average    ____ obese    ____ thin
____ slight     ____ frail    ____ gross

*Mobility*

|                  | Can | Cannot | Cane | Walker | Person | Other |
|------------------|-----|--------|------|--------|--------|-------|
| Amb. Inside      |     |        |      |        |        |       |
| Amb. Outside     |     |        |      |        |        |       |
| Get up from seat |     |        |      |        |        |       |
| Get up from bed  |     |        |      |        |        |       |

*Personal Care*

|          | Independent | Part-Assist. | Total Assist. |
|----------|-------------|--------------|---------------|
| Bathing  |             |              |               |
| Dressing |             |              |               |
| Grooming |             |              |               |
| Feeding  |             |              |               |

*Elimination*

|         | Continent | Occ. Incont. | Incontinent |
|---------|-----------|--------------|-------------|
| Bladder |           |              |             |
| Bowel   |           |              |             |

Uses:
____ catheter
____ "diapers"

*Mental Status*
____ alert      ____ confused/disoriented    ____ hostile
____ forgetful  ____ agitated/restless

*Care Plan*
Tasks of Service Provider
____ shopping
____ cleaning
____ cooking
____ personal care
____ transportation
_____

| Days      | Hours      |
|-----------|------------|
| ____ Mon  | _____ |
| ____ Tues | _____ |
| ____ Wed  | _____ |
| ____ Thurs| _____ |
| ___ Fri   | _____ |
| ____ Sat  | _____ |
| ____ Sun  | _____ |

Comments:
_____
_____
_____
_____
_____
_____
_____

Nurse_____ Telephone # _____

# OUTREACH
## HOMEBOUND PROGRAM
### *Home Assessment*

Name _____

Address _____

Telephone _____

Nearest Contact Person_____ Relationship _____

Telephone _____

Date: _____

## PHYSICAL/MENTAL/MEDICATION/ENVIRONMENT ASSESSMENT

_____

_____

_____

_____

_____

_____

_____

_____

_____

_____

_____

Assessment by: _____

PLAN OF CARE

_____

_____

_____

_____

_____

_____

_____

IMPLEMENTATION OF CARE

_____

_____

_____

_____

_____

_____

_____

_____

_____

# OUTREACH
# HOMEBOUND PROGRAM
*Volunteer Information*

Name_____ Date_____

Address _____ Age _____

_____ Telephone_____

Language Spoken: ____ English ____ Italian ____ Spanish ____ Other_____

I am willing to do:
____ personal care (bathing, dressing)
____ shopping
____ cooking
____ light housekeeping
____ heavy housekeeping
____ laundry
____ transportation (to doctor, shopping)

I would like to volunteer:
____ Part Time
____ Full Time
____ Live-in

____ Monday
____ Tuesday
____ Wednesday
____ Thursday
____ Friday
____ Saturday
____ Sunday

Do you drive a car? _____

I prefer:
____ male client    ____ female client    ____ no preference

Likes:
_____
_____
_____
_____
_____
_____

Dislikes:
_____
_____
_____
_____
_____
_____

Office Comments:_____
_____
_____
_____
_____
_____
_____
_____
_____
_____

| Service Rendered to: | Start | Complete | Excellent | Good | Adequate | Inadeq. | Comments |
|---|---|---|---|---|---|---|---|
| | | | | | | | |
| | | | | | | | |
| | | | | | | | |
| | | | | | | | |
| | | | | | | | |
| | | | | | | | |
| | | | | | | | |
| | | | | | | | |
| | | | | | | | |
| | | | | | | | |
| | | | | | | | |
| | | | | | | | |
| | | | | | | | |
| | | | | | | | |
| | | | | | | | |

Additional Comments: _____

_____

_____

_____

_____

_____

_____

_____

_____

_____

_____

# Chapter 6
# Counseling and Referral

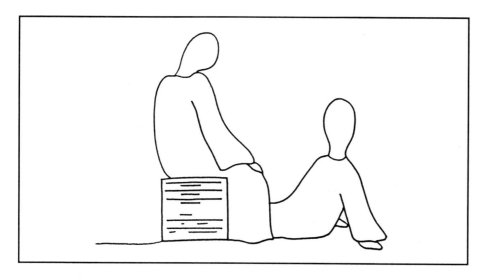

*Lord Jesus, you attracted the blind and the lame, the deaf and the dumb.*

*The woman with the hemorrhage strained to touch your garment, and the Canaanite woman incessantly begged help from you. Men sat by pools and laid on mats before you. Children were presented to you in faith. You, Jesus, blessed them all.*

*Give us, O God, a heart like Jesus. Help us to welcome and assist all who come to Outreach with whatever needs they have. Permit the same power which worked in Jesus to work through us so that the very Spirit of God may be a blessing for all people. In faith and trust we make this prayer, O God, in Jesus' name.*

As Outreach's major conduit for all referrals and concrete services, the counseling and referral program proposes to
    (1) assess the legitimate needs of people;
    (2) help people discover and select appropriate strategies for problem solving on their own behalf;
    (3) emotionally and spiritually support individuals and families in their time of need.
The success of a counseling and referral program rests upon

the interviewing skills of the Outreach director and his or her knowledge of and ability to access local community services.

This chapter will define "counseling" and "referral" from a pastoral perspective. It will offer the reader practical approaches for acquiring the necessary information needed to create and organize selective community information into a resource file whose structuring will foster inter-agency cooperation and networking and facilitate the referral aspects of the program.

Because the scope and practice of the parish's counseling and referral program is defined by Christian theology, it is imperative that Outreach clearly and confidently project the extent of its practice as well as its limitations.

Outreach must interpret for itself and for the community what it is and what it is not. <u>Outreach is not the primary care-giver for people needing physical or mental intervention</u>. Nor is Outreach the principal agent for people procuring entitlements or needing governmental assistance. Outreach and its counseling and referral method are not intended to supplant, duplicate or mimic other community or societal models and services already available to people in need. Rather the parish rightfully maintains itself as the skilled professional addressing people's needs through gospel based service programs. Through compassionate presence, supportive caring, spiritual assistance and counseling, people without distinction can be helped to find direction and the encouragement they need in obtaining skilled health or therapeutic intervention and/or treatment.

The counseling and referral program involves sensitivity and gentleness and aims (a) to let people know that they are accepted as they are and (b) to assist them with emotional and/or spiritual primary care. The program involves a face to face encounter with a variety of individuals, each with his or her own diverse needs.

Outreach's counseling and referral program requires consistency (significant time commitment), professionalism, and a thorough knowledge of area resources to competently guide and direct people toward the procurement of appropriate outside intervention. Lay (non-professional) volunteers and even professionals who by their experience are well aware of the necessity of a consistent and substantial time investment do not usually volunteer for counseling and referral program work. Counseling and referral volunteers rather are the people who support others in their recovery and healing by ministering to them through other concrete Outreach programs such as food, bereavement, housing programs, etc., to which the people are referred through the counseling and referral program.

Outreach's counseling and referral program attracts people with spiritual and communication difficulties and persons who have not been able to adequately address their problem(s) because of no or insufficient knowledge of the social systems and networks available to help them. Refugees, illegal aliens and people with AIDS and addictions often come to Outreach frightened and/or exhausted from having unsuccessfully made their rounds of agency and/or government assistance programs each with its own confusing, sometimes repetitive and conflicting criteria. For these people the parish's counseling and referral program becomes a non-threatening, confidential and safe haven for people to emotionally relieve themselves and to explore factors contributing to their difficulty.

The director's ability to listen to people in need is qualitatively essential to the counseling and referral program. Through interested and skilled listening, the director arrives at an understanding and a clearer appreciation of the person and his or her presenting problem and contributing history. The Outreach director can help people by using what he or she has heard to help the presenter recall events, clarify facts and relive responses and by offering subsequent advice and referral to primary care givers.

In summary, Parish Outreach strives to create and provide Christian programs of compassion in action which complement and buttress the services of primary care givers. Legitimate unmet needs of people can be holistically and competently addressed through cooperation between the parish and other professionals skilled in their own areas of expertise. A parish so organized consistently offers programs of compassion in action, which are supportive to persons/families emotionally labile, exhausted and/or depressed because of personal circumstances or possibly because of the experiences of systemic injustices and consequent inherent dehumanization. Through professed application of the gospel, people can be strengthened to persist through the morass of social mechanisms toward resolving their problems and acquiring their rightful entitlements. Knowledge of the local community, its people, its businesses and its agencies is essential to such practical support. This knowledge will foster a spirit of inter-agency friendliness and cooperation and ensure appropriate referrals from the parish. Inter-agency networking further presents an opportunity for Outreach to extend its Christian influence beyond the parish and its boundaries, ultimately influencing neighborhoods to become more caring communities (see Chapter 8 on consciousness raising). Knowing and being able to use neighborhood services makes the parish's Outreach counseling (discussing options and the giving of advice) and referral (guiding the individual to primary care providers or to concrete parish and neighborhood services) program credible and effective.

While the initial acquiring of community information, creating a resource file and beginning inter-agency networking might seem to be an overwhelming task, the practical approach which follows can make the job relatively easy. One must remember, however, that the proposed path to learning is a process that will take time. To rush will jeopardize an otherwise sure foundation to inter-agency knowledge and parish-agency cooperation.

## Practical Learning and Networking

Every neighborhood community has identified agencies, organizations and groups, each retaining its own purpose and generally consisting of people who are highly committed to the needs of local residents. Area providers are usually eager to educate the community about their service and they are generally open to participate in and share local community information. Phone contacts and selected personal visits between the director of the organization or program and the Outreach director are therefore welcomed and prove to be mutually informative and helpful. Such personal contacts and/or visits enhance Outreach's planning toward meeting legitimate local needs without duplication of service within the community. They help the parish and the agency establish realistic cooperation, accurate inter-agency networking, and mutual assistance, including the development of a useful resource file for the parish and updated information about Outreach for the cooperating agency. To establish a sense of professionalism, equality, credibility and pride for both agency and Outreach programs, contact between directors is encouraged.

To prepare for these suggested contacts by phone or visit, "tools of the trade" are presented here as well as a guide to help the reader discover how to identify and locate such important local groups and resources.

Directories and local newspapers aid the discovery of the local neighborhood offices closest to the parish. Commonly used directories which easily access names, addresses and phone numbers include:

- the local yellow pages (immediately uncovers local community organizations and groups as well as religious institutions and churches);

- the white and yellow phone directories (used for discovering services beyond the local neighborhood);

- the diocesan directory (guides one to all Catholic Institutions and services);

- the reverse directory which is a street address and numerical directory. It provides the reader with addresses and family names of occupants, house to house, and street to street. This is a priceless reference for gleaning the neighborhood's ethnic makeup and for use in door to door mailings or ministries (the reverse directory can generally be purchased for a modest price from the local "Yellow Book Company").

Local newspapers convey the flavor of the neighborhood, its current concerns and plans. The information provided through these written materials includes short descriptions of services (support groups, health services, nutritional information services, youth opportunities, counseling offerings, etc.) along with telephone numbers to obtain further information. These newspapers cost nothing when procured in supermarkets, libraries, banks, post offices, and other public buildings:

- the county newspaper (for resources and information beyond the local neighborhood);

- the neighborhood newspaper (for the most proximate services and providers).

To create a resource file, purchase index cards or an alphabetical card organizer. Using the tools presented below, record name, address, telephone number, and short description of services on individual cards (later to be alphabetized). The following pages offer the reader a guide to organizations and services essential to a viable parish resource file.

## Neighborhood Organizations and Services

    Commerce
    Community Boards (or governing body)
    Fire Department
    Jobs
    Police Department
    Real Estate
    Transportation
    Vocational Services
    Youth Services

Information one wants to discover from such groups includes the neighborhood's stability, its ethnicity, the median age, and the socio-economic status. The library reference section contains resource materials including the latest census, description of neighborhood needs and improvement goals such as plans for building housing units and establishing day care or youth services and proposals for improving health care. The Health Systems Management Reference Manual can also be particularly helpful.

## Neighborhood Health (Physical-Mental) Services

    Alzheimer Resource Center
    Disabled
    Health Related Facilities
    Health Department
    Home Care
    Hospitals
    Maternity
    Medicare
    Mental Health
    Nurses (Also look under VNS)
    Nursing Homes
    Physicians
    Psychologists
    Public Health Services
    Retarded Persons Services
    Sex Information and Counseling

Hospitals, clinics and nursing homes are usually easily identifiable in the local community and can quickly become a part of Outreach's resource file. Also of import are the nearest community health department and the visiting nurse service which provide early post-natal home care to mother and baby and health assistance to homebound people. Mental health and counseling providers are essential to the resource file as are any local support groups for things such as chemical dependency, abusive relationships, etc.

## Neighborhood Human Services

Adoption
Adult Protective Services
Aging (Department of)
Alcoholics Anonymous
Alzheimer Resource Center
Battered Women (also look under Abused)
Child Abuse
Disabled
Drug Abuse and Addiction
Eviction Assistance
Food Assistance
Food Stamps
Immigration and Naturalization
Jobs
Legal Counseling
Medicaid
Men's Shelter
Psychologist
Public Assistance
Retarded Persons Services
Senior Citizens
Shelters
Social and Human Services
Social Security
Sex Information and Counseling
Women's Services
Women's Shelter
Welfare

City agencies exist to help people with their health and welfare entitlements (e.g., Medicare, Medicaid, SSI, Public Assistance, Food Stamps, WIC, ADC, etc.). Outreach must know the nearest office and the appropriate eligibility criteria. Making incorrect referrals aggravates relationships between an agency and Outreach. Knowledge, on the other hand, will buttress parish relations in the local community and will help witness to the sincerity of a church which aims to be respectful and caring of agencies as well as individuals.

## Neighborhood Educational Services

City College
Day Care
Education (Elementary/High)

Child care, grade and high schools, colleges and universities are important resources. Besides providing generic education to its students, these institutions offer help in other areas such as parental guidance, courses on coping with stress, and health care, English as a second language, vocational training, etc. Also of note and value is that professionals involved in education will often offer substantial support to an Outreach program perhaps by volunteering to offer mini-courses to parishioners, donating food and toys to the needy, encouraging student volunteers, etc.

## Neighborhood Religious Organizations and Services

Religious Organizations
Catholic Charities

Last but far from least are the local churches, synagogues, and Catholic Charities neighborhood involvements. A special bond exists between parish Outreach and Christian churches in particular because of the shared theology of service based on the good Samaritan gospel story. It is with the local churches that Outreach can ecumenically plan and work for the unification and revitalization of the neighborhood through compassionate service. Inviting the involvement of non-Christian people and congregations of worship in the initial efforts of parish Outreach is best achieved by direct contact between the pastor and the Outreach director.

Having established an Outreach identity with a positive image in the local community, possessing basic knowledge of eligibility criteria and with basic resource file in place, counseling and referral can become formalized as an Outreach program.

A simple narrative form (see page 77) can help the Outreach director remember individuals, circumstances and plans of care so as to assist a growing number of people. Case studies will later be used to demonstrate usage of this simple form which is designed to record basic and helpful information: the presenting person, the address and phone number. The form also provides room for the date and a brief description of the person's stature, appearance, purpose of the visit, etc.

Mounds of paperwork are not only unnecessary, but can

eventually become burdensome. Simply note any divergence from the normal (e.g., an unsteady gait, limp, scar, speech or hearing limitation, etc.) and indicate the presenting problem along with Outreach's plan of care, viz., advice given, referrals suggested, etc. Such details will help the Outreach director recall each presenter in the event of return visits and/or increasing numbers of presenters. Use the resource file to refer the person for help when necessary. If Outreach has already developed programs for food, bereavement, finances, etc., the person can be internally referred and served by the parish's Outreach's volunteers.

Counseling and referral require practice and skill. Keep in mind that the parish's counseling and referral program is not a social work model. Listen compassionately and be secure in making appropriate referrals. Where there are referral questions on the part of the director, talk with the local human or health service (agency) director/person who was the initial contact with the parish Outreach director. Learning is a daily occurrence within a parish's Outreach program. Remember that appropriate referrals are safe and professional. Use and reap the benefits of Outreach's resource file.

The following true stories demonstrate:

(1) A simple documentation style as suggested.

(2) A sampling of various presenters

    (a) Abused mentally ill woman

    (b) Pregnant homeless teenager

    (c) Family burned out of their home

    (d) Single parent

(3) Outreach's networking with local service providers, government programs, health and human services and/or providing concrete parish assistance.

(4) Pastoral/spiritual intervention as necessary/appropriate.

# AN ABUSED MENTALLY ILL PERSON

*PRESENTER:*

Mrs. V, 68 years old, came to the Outreach office without appointment. "Bag lady" appearance, very unkempt, in great need of hygienic attention. No teeth but is able to articulate clearly. Twitching of the mouth, frequent repetition and rapid speech. Appears to need mental health attention. She states that her husband deserted her 10 years ago and that her son with whom she lives abuses her.

We discussed several approaches to deal with the abusive son but Mrs. V states this has been a long standing problem that remains out of control. She seemed to have no hope for any modification of his behavior. We talked about protective services, an idea which she was willing to try. Mrs. V has hard time centering any conversation.

*ASSESSMENT:*

Subjective:

      (1) seems depressed (e.g., hygiene, hopeless feelings)

      (2) Ability to follow through with own plan of care?

Objective:

      (1) own mental health

      (2) son's abusiveness

*INITIAL PLAN:*

Referral by phone made to protective services from Outreach.

*OUTCOME:*

Within 48 hours, the caseworker for adult protective service made a visit to Mrs. V's home at which time Mrs. V informed the caseworker that her son had moved out the week before with no forwarding address. Adult protective services informed Outreach that this case was closed.

*FOLLOW-UP PLAN:*

Outreach contacted a local mobile crisis team of mental health professionals who visited Mrs. V at home.

*EVALUATION:*

Through the intervention of the local mobile crisis team, Mrs. V was hospitalized for physical as well as mental attention and treatment. Outreach remains available to assist Mrs. V upon discharge.

# A PREGNANT HOMELESS TEENAGER

*PRESENTER:*

Ms. R, unmarried, pregnant, 17 years old. Walked in to Outreach office. States she is 7 months pregnant and homeless. Spent previous 7 months of pregnancy living two weeks at a time with various friends. Says she used to live with her mother but was forced to leave prior to her pregnancy because of her mother's serious abuse of drugs. Denies any use of drugs before or since her pregnancy. Has never received pre-natal care. Is concerned over her general unpreparedness for a baby. No place to live after its birth. Ms. R's 19 year old boy friend and father of the baby is jobless. Ms. R indicates his desire to help her.

*ASSESSMENT:*

Subjective:

    (1) Expresses concern for the basic needs of herself and her unborn child.

    (2) Shows signs of genuine motivation and determination to solve her problem.

Objective:

    (1) needs prenatal care.

    (2) feels unprepared to be a mother.

    (3) homeless.

*PLAN:*

Referred to:

    (1) Birthright for pre-natal counseling and help;

    (2) perinatal council for government entitlements including public assistance, medi-caid, food stamps, and the woman, infants and children program;

    (3) the nearest religiously sponsored program for housing pregnant homeless teenagers.

*OUTCOME:*

Ms. R followed through with all the referrals. Made application for public assistance which entitled her to be temporarily housed in religiously sponsored program until 6 months after baby's birth.

*EVALUATION:*

Ms. R had a healthy baby boy. She lived in the referred home for several weeks after the baby's birth. With government entitlements, Ms. R was able to rent a small apartment into which she, her boyfriend and the baby moved. She and her mate procured part-time jobs, staggering the hours of work so as to provide the baby with care. The situation remains precarious. Outreach stands by ready to assist should that be necessary in the future.

# A FAMILY BURNED OUT OF THEIR HOME

*PRESENTER:*

Outreach alerted to the plight of Family P by a succession of phone calls from neighbors and the principal of the parish school. Family P's home destroyed by fire.

Family consists of working parents, 7 children ages 1 to 11 years. Two of the children attend the parish school. Through the children Outreach learned that the family was living with their aunt (the mother's sister) who also lived in the neighborhood.

Outreach phoned the aunt and spoke with her and Mrs. P both of whom agreed to and welcomed an Outreach visit to the home. Mr. and Mrs. P and their children were present. They expressed their shock and disbelief over their tremendous loss and were grateful for the lives of themselves and all their children. Everything including their clothing, school uniforms, and furniture was destroyed by the fire. They stated that they contacted their insurance company and were waiting to hear how they would be assisted.

*ASSESSMENT:*

Subjective:

    (1) family unit intact.

    (2) supportive extended family.

Objective:

    (1) grieving family.

    (2) basic needs—food, clothing, finances.

*PLAN:*

    (1) Immediate referrals to:

        (a) The food program (Outreach) for on the spot and ongoing food assistance.

        (b) The clothing program of a local church.

        (c) Direct financial assistance from Outreach. (St. Vincent de Paul Society)

    (2) Outreach offered the family the supportive opportunity of meeting and venting with another family who had the experience of being burned out of their home.

*EVALUATION:*

With Outreach support and referrals, the family, assisted by their fire insurance and finances from their own work places, was able to procure temporary shelter during the many months of the rebuilding of their original home. Through the food and clothing assistance offered by the parish Outreach program this family was further able to save money for housing costs, payment of bills, and other necessary expenses. Mr. and Mrs. P chose not to meet the other family with a similar history of loss and grief. They expressed much gratitude to God for their safety and the generous response of help from many sources.

It took over 18 months for Mr. and Mrs. P to be resettled in their rebuilt home. The family sent cards of thanks to the pastor of the parish, to Outreach and to the school.

# A SINGLE PARENT

*PRESENTER:*

Ms. T has disheveled hair, mismatched clothing. Appears restless and anxious. A single mother. Recently and secretly moved with her 5 year old son from Ohio to NY to escape her husband who abuses cocaine and alcohol. Admits to abusing alcohol at times. She is 27 years old. States she never felt close to her own family all of whom live in the states of Ohio and Florida.

Ms. T lives in the attic of a one family dwelling rent-free in exchange for caring for the elderly female owner of the house. Has applied for public assistance, Medicaid, and food stamps for herself and her son.

Ms. T expresses inability to adequately clothe and feed herself and her son. She also admits to losing patience with her child and fears abusing him. She states concern over his loss of a father image. When asked "Where has God been for you during these difficult times?" Ms. T fought back tears and said she didn't know how to begin to rediscover God in her life.

*ASSESSMENT:*

Subjective: Ms. T seems to:

> Have good insight into her problem.
> Be motivated toward assisting self.

Objective: Needs

> (a) Food
> (b) Clothing
> (c) Father image for son
> (d) Loses patience with son
> (e) Occasional abuse of alcohol

*PLAN:*

Referred to:

> (1) Food program (Outreach) for weekly food assistance
> (2) Child care program (Outreach)
> (3) the nearest "clothing closet" with a voucher from Outreach requesting that Ms. T and her son be served at no cost
> (4) parenting classes offered by a local hospital
> (5) local AA meeting sites
> (6) Prayer corner program (Outreach)

*OUTCOME:*

Ms. T regularly utilizes referrals for food, child care, and AA, and occasionally seeks help with clothing, parenting classes and Prayer Corner.

*EVALUATION:*

Supported by parish Outreach, Ms. T's ability to procure basic necessities (food and clothing) for herself and her son eased some of her daily anxieties. Through the parish Outreach child care program a parish family (mother, father, and two female children ages 4 and 6) volunteered to watch Ms. T's son each weekend (Saturday and Sunday) at no cost. Besides being motivated to assist Ms. T and her son this family believed that the little boy would provide a pleasant and broadening experience for their own children.

This arrangement offered the boy a positive male and family experience. Ms. T acquired two days' respite which she used to ride a bicycle, take walks and/or go to the AA meetings and occasionally to a parent support group. Ms. T's appearance markedly improved. She has less of a problem remaining sober and she admitted to having a more pleasant and patient relationship with her son. After acquiring government entitlements, Ms. T moved to a small neighborhood apartment. Through the Outreach employment program Ms. T procured a daytime job housekeeping. Eventually she became more independent from government assistance and from the frequency of the food and clothing programs of the parish. Her son remained in the weekend child care setting of the said family. Ms. T is presently considering taking night courses at a nearby college for certification as a nurse's assistant.

The effect of Outreach can be real and profound for many people who ask the parish for help in time of need. The following excerpts speak of the overall gratitude of people who have been assisted through a Parish Counseling and Referral Program.

"It is I who always break silence with a prayer. 'Jesus, bless Outreach and make the path straight before them because they have dared to touch a broken heart, to heal it with your love.' Thank you."

"I truly can't find the words to express my appreciation to Outreach. Please continue to pray for us. There can never be any way I can repay you. Thank you again."

"You have made a beautiful difference in my life. Our family was in deep despair. God chose Outreach to answer our prayer. Prayers for all of you will never cease."

| | OUTREACH |
|---|---|

Name _____

Address _____

Telephone _____

| Date | Narrative |
|---|---|
| | |
| | |
| | |
| | |
| | |
| | |
| | |
| | |
| | |
| | |
| | |
| | |
| | |
| | |
| | |
| | |
| | |
| | |
| | |
| | |
| | |

# Chapter 7
# Food

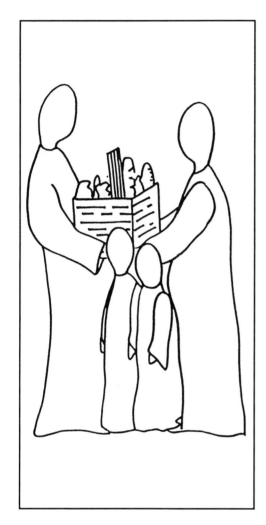

*All powerful Father, God of goodness, you provide for all your creation. Give us an effective love for our brothers and sisters who suffer from lack of food. Help us to continue to do all we can to relieve their hunger. May your body and blood be the food which sustains our ministry to the needy. Send your Spirit upon us to strengthen us in the prayers and the good works we do on behalf of the hungry. Give all of us a growing awareness of our unity with Christ who had compassion and love for all who suffer. We ask these gifts from you, Father, in the name of Jesus Christ your Son, who lives and reigns with you in the unity of the Holy Spirit, One God, forever and ever. Amen.*

This chapter will detail the gradual stages of a many-faceted food program whose aim is to assess and to help provide for the basic unmet nutritional and food needs of neighborhood people in distress. The parts of the food program discussed in these pages focus upon food distribution but also include information regarding the raising, stocking, cooking, separating and delivering of food.

This chapter addresses the eventual delicate combination of the food program components and the fine-tuned organization which makes possible the "feeding" of hundreds of people while respecting cultural differences and nutritional health and family size. The psychological and Christian responses to people who abuse or attempt to abuse the goodness and generosity of a parish's food program by selling food for drugs or for other unhealthful reasons will also be explored.

A parish food program usually begins prior to any formalized planning and very simply. It consists in giving sandwiches or canned foods to the hungry (food distribution) who present themselves to the church or Outreach office asking for food assistance.

This is the initial alert to any parish that hungry or nutritionally indigent people live nearby. Included are single parents, runaway youths, homeless women and men, families burned out of their homes, unemployed people and others. Another less obvious and forgotten population are the undernourished, homebound frail elderly or the ill person who is unable to shop for food necessities and who may not be able to prepare proper meals. All unattended elderly ill people need nutritional attention.

While some need help sporadically, other people require regular food assistance. The initial groundwork for program development prior to determining parameters rests with the food raising, stocking, and distribution strategies. The two most immediate and effective approaches include: the use of the parish bulletin and the purchase of inviting and eye catching food receptacles (barrels).

The parish bulletin should be regularly utilized to inform parishioners and the community at large of the food needs of local people. Through the periodic updating of its readers the parish bulletin can become an effective consciousness raising tool which will assist in the recruiting of volunteers to help feed the hungry who come to the church for assistance. In addition to bulletin blurbs, large pastel colored barrels can be purchased, labeled "Outreach: Food for the Poor" and placed by each of the church entrances. These receptacles are a constant visual alert to parishioners reminding them of the ongoing food needs of people and inviting their compassion by way of food donations.

Consistent and regular use of the bulletin and the continual presence of the food containers at all church entrances will increase parishioners' awareness of the needs of the area's hungry. Along with questions about the real existence of hungry people in the neighborhood, expect

(a) expressions of shock and/or concern from individuals in the parish congregation;

(b) a trickle of food donations;

(c) the tug of volunteerism from a few people who will offer to assist giving food to the hungry.

Now is the time to:

(a) designate a small area for storing the donated food (food stocking)—this will help to organize and simplify the distribution of food;

(b) receive all volunteers into the food program following strategies suggested and outlined in Chapter 1.

At this point the reader has become aware of the basic components of planning and implementing a simple food program, viz. the raising, stocking, consciousness raising and food raising (bulletin and food receptacles) as well as an unsophisticated system for food distribution. Before discussing the gradual planning necessary for developing a Food Program, and prior to determining program boundaries and eligibility criteria, one must consider the methods for dealing with actual and potential food program abusers.

A category of users of the food distribution program to which the director must be alert and realistic are the real and potential abusers of the food program. These are people who are motivated by a drug, alcohol, or other addictive behavior and who may have the intention of selling the canned food items to support their addictive habit. Because justice dictates that the parish distribute donated food wisely and charitably, potential abusers must not be allowed to manipulate or dupe the parish's food program. Shrewd planning on the part of the parish can ensure that abusive or manipulative people are not rejected but rather can find understanding and concrete assistance with any real need for food which they may have.

The challenge to actively and wisely provide for people's food needs without the possibility of their abusing the generosity of food donors is met by providing food which cannot be sold. Serving sandwiches or prepared food, for example, rather than offering canned foods to persons meets whatever legitimate food need they may have but will deter return visits by people whose food needs are not based on legitimate need. Should Outreach be regularly visited by such individuals, the director may want to purchase a small refrigerator to store prepared sandwiches. A volunteer or two may occasionally prepare a cooked meal such as a tuna or vegetable casserole for the "needy person/family." This can also be stored in the small refrigerator for quick access to the presenter. Because sandwiches and cooked foods in aluminum tins or air tight baggies are usually not saleable, the end of potential abusers will be thwarted and they will usually quickly fall away from the parish's food distribution program. (Note that food cooking and food separation component has been introduced into the implementation of the food distribution program.)

Uncomplicated successful beginnings can result in program stability and growth. Planning for this developing food program becomes expedient and essential. Parameters and criteria must be set in place before advancing the program.

Because the amount of food needed to be raised (food raising) and the number of volunteers which will be needed to maintain the program (food stocking, cooking, separation, distribution) depend upon the number of recipients to be served (food distribution), one must decide upon eligibility criteria at the outset of simple program implementation. Program parameters can be a numerical decision to accept a set number of recipients into the program or it can be a decision made based upon geographical boundaries. Either approach targets the population to be served. Examples will help to clarify.

"Parish A" might elect "parishioners only" to its food program or it may decide that the parish boundaries make for eligibility. Planning a food program for this parish will have a more limited scope than "Parish B" whose boundaries may be less restrictive. "Parish B" for example may want its parameters to extend to the entire local neighborhood. Parameters significantly affect the size and the development of the food program.

Besides deciding upon specific geographical boundaries, the characteristics of the circumstances of potential recipients must be regarded when planning a food program. Answers to such questions as: Will the program be aimed at crisis intervention? Or will it be intended to support the chronically indigent? For how long? Weeks? Months? Years? will help determine program usage and its scope. Crisis intervention implies a recipient's short term usage of a smaller Food Program vs. a larger Food Program designed to address the ongoing or long term needs of the chronically indigent.

To assist the reader with the stages of planning and program growth the following paragraphs will refer to the development of an actual successful food program. Note the specific program parameters and the eligibility criteria and be encouraged to modify, adapt and use the frames of reference presented here to suit the aims and circumstances of your particular parish and community. The approaches to planning a food program are as diverse as its planners.

The following pages focus upon the food distribution aspect of the food program around which all other food program facets revolve. Note this demonstration program's pre-determined parameters: (a) the geographical scope is inclusive of the local neighborhood, (b) circumstances of eligibility are determined within the parish's counseling and referral program, (c) the program intends to support people in crisis as well as the chronically indigent.

People eligible for food assistance from the parish are those who are unable to adequately feed themselves or their families because of individual/family circumstances such as:

- Marital desertion/separation
- Job loss
- Sudden illness
- Unforeseen bills (acute, not chronic occurrence)
- Delayed reception of pension or government assistance
- Persons who have applied for public assistance, food stamps and/or other governmental assistance and are awaiting their first payment
- Persons without eligibility for government assistance, for example, illegal aliens, legal aliens awaiting legal status, etc.
- Persons with a fixed income, including the homebound ill
- The homeless

People are provided weekly with one week's supply of food. Food assistance is permitted for one year during which time financial management and other problem solving is encouraged and supervised by the counseling and referral program. (The counseling and referral program refers recipients to agencies for primary care and concrete help in areas which contribute to their dependence on food assistance.)

Before continuing to detail this demonstration program and presuming growth in the numbers of people requesting food, an increasing amount of food donations and the need for additional volunteers, one must plan for program development by (a) widening the consciousness raising circle beyond the parish and (b) procuring and organizing the needed volunteers.

To do this the Outreach director may want to consider setting up a meeting by invitation (see sample on next page) with the pastors of other Christian neighborhood churches. There an overview may be given of the kinds of people coming to the church for assistance. Specifically focus on the needs of the area's hungry who often have other basic needs such as clothing, employment, etc. Invite their responses. Ask for their own history and approaches. Suggest Outreach's willingness to cooperate with other Christians to help meet other people's needs. Specific planning at the first meeting, although ideal, is not essential to Outreach's aim. The main purpose of the meeting is to raise the consciousness of pastors and their congregations to the food and other basic needs of local people. Capitalize upon these initial consciousness raising efforts by placing each pastor on Outreach's

Dear Pastor,

Over the past six months our parish Outreach program has assisted an increasing number of people coming to our church requesting food for themselves and/or their families. Respecting your church's approach to people in need and interested in cooperating with you to better serve people in legitimate need, Outreach invites you or your representative to join with me and other neighborhood pastors on Day—Date—Time—Place—to share your history and experience in addressing the food and other basic needs of the local people assisted by our churches.

I ask God's blessing upon us and the work we do in Jesus' name.

Sincerely,

Outreach Director

mailing list for reception of the parish's weekly bulletin. Highlight the Outreach column.

The meeting of pastors just described, coupled with the continual use of the parish bulletin and the food receptacles at church entrances, will continue to attract people, inviting them to offer their service to the food program as volunteers. Consistent with the principles of volunteer theology, psychology, and methodology (see Chapter 1), individually interview and welcome each person wanting to assist the food program. Use the volunteer log book to maintain a record of the growing number of food pantry volunteers. Program design determines the time and tasks of volunteerism. Detailing the demonstration food distribution program will clarify.

The food distribution program aspires to recognize and respect the diverse backgrounds and circumstances of individuals and families requesting food assistance while honoring the sensitivity and safety of food distribution program volunteers. A dual distribution system which distinguishes between users (registered recipients) and abusers (periodic recipients) makes the food distribution program function smoothly and safely for all. The reader will observe that both arrangements are distinct, albeit complementary.

To appreciate the organization, approach and rationale of each method, one must purposefully distinguish between food recipients who are the "one timers" or sporadic users; people who are at high risk for security breeches, such as persons who are heavy into the drug scene, drifters, abusers of the food distribution system, or persons who because of overt or suspect behavior jeopardize the safety of volunteers; and those who require regular (weekly, monthly, quarterly, etc.) food assistance (registered recipients). Organize the program by purchasing two loose leaf binders. Label one "Food Distribution Program/Periodic Recipients" and the other "Food Distribution Program/Registered Recipients."

Use a food program registration form (see sample, page 91) to help maintain a simple record of name, date, number in household and language spoken. This is the minimal, essential food distribution record keeping of the high risk and/or periodic recipient. Place the completed form alphabetically in the loose leaf binder labeled "Periodic Recipients." These logged individuals can receive food as needed from donations stored in a small room or from the refrigerated sandwiches or prepared foods.

The Outreach approach to the non-abuser and to non-threatening registered recipients requiring ongoing food assistance is more challenging. This course demands creative program planning, and tailored record keeping. The explanation of some useful tools follows.

*A Food Program Registration Form* (see sample, page 91) records all the necessary information for people needing regular food assistance. This form documents the family name, which could be anonymous, the number in the household and the person's/family's native language. Each family member's age is listed in the left margin. Place the completed forms alphabetically in the loose leaf binder labeled "Registered Recipients."

All information on the *Food Program Distribution Guidelines* (see sample, pages 93–94) is for "Office Use Only." Entries are made by the Outreach director or a knowledgeable volunteer. The food distribution guide is designed to provide nutritionally balanced meals. It also aims to assist food distribution volunteers in determining the cultural kinds of food the family might need or be interested in as well as the amount of food to be issued. For example, the ages shown may be 36, 28 and five months. Formula or baby food would be appropriate for this family. Family ages 48, 42, 19, 17, and 15 alerts volunteers to the probability of teenagers with ravenous appetites. Thus this family would receive more food and a different type than the aforementioned family with a baby. The *Food Program Distribution Form* (see sample, pages 95–96) encourages the food distribution volunteers to actually document the types and amount of food given to the presenter based on the distribution guide. This helps volunteers to nutritionally assist families in the selection of healthful food combinations.

The reader should notice that the food distribution process is completely dependent upon the utilization and organization of volunteers.

Consciousness raising helps to attract volunteers. Continue to use the bulletin to describe every step of the planning and development of the food program. Some people already bringing food items to the food barrels on a weekly or even daily basis may now offer to assist in other ways. A volunteer preference form (see sample, page 97) can be distributed to parishioners as an enclosure in the parish bulletin. This form suggests volunteerism for any and all aspects of Outreach's food program, including the raising, stocking, cooking and delivery of food. Some forms may be left at the church and rectory entrances. Consistent with the principles of volunteer theology and psychology (see Chapter 1), individually interview and welcome each person volunteering for the food program. Glean the amount and frequency of time that they are willing to give to any part of the food program. Enter their names alphabetically according to their interest in the food program. The volunteer book should also reflect people willing to assist in the delivery aspect of a food program. These will be people willing to prepare and/or deliver prepared bags of food or cooked hot meals to the homebound sick or elderly.

The proposed volunteer schedule is helpful for organizing food distribution volunteers. The schedule divides the distribution time (e.g., 3 to 8 P.M.) into "hour slots" and provides space to assign two to three volunteers per slot (see sample volunteer schedule, page 99).

The sample schedule chooses Wednesday as the arbitrarily chosen day for regular food distribution. The sample also reflects hours—3 to 8 P.M.—which would be convenient to people picking up children from the nearby schools and/or for people who must work during the day and are not available to come to the food distribution center except during evening hours.

On the reverse of the page is the name and telephone of each volunteer. It is the responsibility of the distributing volunteer to cover for herself/himself in case of absenteeism. The last resort of the volunteer is to call the Outreach director in the event that a substitute cannot be found.

With the schedule in place, call individual volunteers by phone to tell them of their time slot and to be sure that the time and the convenience of their donation have been respected. Most likely some alterations will have to be made. A food distribution procedure for registered recipients follows the organization of volunteers. Here is a sample procedure:

```
PARISH OUTREACH
FOOD DISTRIBUTION PROCEDURE

1. Person presents self at food distribution door
2. Name of person is checked against registration book
   (a) If person is not registered
       1. prepare a bag of food for that day
       2. instruct person to return to Outreach the following morning for assessment through
          the counseling and referral program
   (b) If person is registered
       1. person enters food distribution center
       2. person chooses his or her own type of food according to Individualized Distribution
          Guidelines (see sample, pages 93–94)
       3. volunteer assists persons in selecting and bagging food
       4. volunteer escorts person from the food distribution center
3. Volunteer completes Food Distribution Form (see sample, pages 95–96)
4. Volunteer enters date, time, signature on Registration Form (see sample, page 91)
```

A copy of the procedure should be sent with the volunteer schedule and a letter (see sample, next page) to each volunteer.

When volunteers come to Outreach for their orientation, remind them that the food distribution procedure is for the regular recipients of food. Tell them that in order to minimize confusion and upset, periodic recipients are advised to receive food any day of the week exclusive of Wednesday (food distribution day). These periodic recipients of food receive the non-saleable goods as previously discussed.

Point out to volunteers that these regular recipients of the food distribution program are registered in a loose leaf binder by way of the food registration form. This "registration book" is kept in the food distribution center for use by all volunteers during food distribution hours.

Advise volunteers of the specifics of program functioning: The recipient comes to the food distribution center (food storage area). The stated name is checked against the registration book. The name of the recipient is either present or not.

*If the recipient's name is not present (registered) in the registration book: either the person has never been registered to receive food from the parish or the individual/family was once registered but has been removed by the director pending a reevaluation.* In either case the person is greeted at the food distribution center door but may not enter the center. This non-registered person is

Dear Food Distribution Volunteer,

I want to tell each one of you personally how very pleased I am about the offering of your time and talents to help distribute food to needy people through Outreach. How delighted I am to share this special ministry with you! Welcome!

Enclosed please find

    a Food Distribution Procedure

    the Volunteer Schedule

These enclosures will be discussed with you when you come for your first hour of volunteerism. We promise to give you a simple yet thorough orientation and answer all the questions you may have about this important ministry.

I thank you for responding to people in need as I ask God's blessings upon you and your family.

Sincerely in Christ,

Outreach Director

---

given food to last that day only. The individual is then advised to return to Outreach the next day to be assessed or reevaluated for food assistance through the counseling and referral program.

*If the recipient's name is present in the registration book, the person is eligible for a week's supply of food.* The recipient enters the food distribution center where a volunteer meets and greets the person at the food distribution center door. Once in the distribution center, the person chooses his or her own type of food, according to the individualized Distribution Guidelines for that particular individual/family (see sample, pages 93–94). This form assists good nutritional practices and educates as to the food groups and nutritional values. It records the recipient's name and the individualized amount of food in each food category that will meet the specific needs of each family. Take the "Milk Group" as an example. The form indicates that a family of two adults would be entitled to at least two quarts of powdered milk per week. A family of two adults and two small children reflects an allotment of six quarts of milk, such as condensed, evaporated or baby formula. This approach is carried out in all other food groups as well.

A volunteer assists the person in selecting, bagging and carrying food and escorts the person to and from the food distribution center door. Volunteers then use the actual distribution form to indicate the amount and type of food given. The food program Registration Form is used to record the time the person was served in the food distribution center. The transaction is finalized by the volunteer's signature.

Volunteers in the food distribution center can also be utilized to prepare bags of food for elderly or sick homebound persons who names also appear in the registration book. Once the bags are prepared, other volunteers willing to deliver prepared packages can be called upon to give their service.

People willing to prepare hot meals for sick or homebound persons can be guided by the hot meals assessment guide (see sample, page 101) which can be completed by phone by volunteers. This guide assists volunteers in cooking inviting meals which conform to the homebound's dietary restrictions and preferences.

A parish food program need not be complicated. Program growth is generally gradual. This chapter provides the reader with ideas and tools which can prove helpful at each stage of program development. The organization described in this chapter can make it possible to feed great numbers of people compassionately.

# OUTREACH
# FOOD PROGRAM
## *Registration Form*

Family Name _____    Date _____

Number in Household _____    Language _____

### *Use of Food Distribution Center*

| Ages | Date | Time | Volunteer's Signature | Date | Time | Volunteer's Signature |
|------|------|------|------------------------|------|------|------------------------|
|  |  |  |  |  |  |  |
|  |  |  |  |  |  |  |
|  |  |  |  |  |  |  |
|  |  |  |  |  |  |  |
|  |  |  |  |  |  |  |
|  |  |  |  |  |  |  |
|  |  |  |  |  |  |  |
|  |  |  |  |  |  |  |
|  |  |  |  |  |  |  |
|  |  |  |  |  |  |  |
|  |  |  |  |  |  |  |
|  |  |  |  |  |  |  |
|  |  |  |  |  |  |  |
|  |  |  |  |  |  |  |
|  |  |  |  |  |  |  |
|  |  |  |  |  |  |  |
|  |  |  |  |  |  |  |
|  |  |  |  |  |  |  |
|  |  |  |  |  |  |  |
|  |  |  |  |  |  |  |
|  |  |  |  |  |  |  |
|  |  |  |  |  |  |  |
|  |  |  |  |  |  |  |

# OUTREACH
# FOOD PROGRAM
## *Distribution Guidelines*

Family Name: _____          FOR OFFICE USE

| CATEGORY | AMOUNT | COMMENTS |
|---|---|---|
| *Milk* | | |
|   Powdered | _____ | _____ |
|   Evaporated/Condensed | _____ | _____ |
| | | |
| *Meat/Protein* | | |
|   Cans—Meat | _____ | _____ |
|   Cans—Fish | _____ | _____ |
|   Pasta/Noodles with | _____ | _____ |
|     Spaghetti Sauce *or* | _____ | _____ |
|     Tomato Sauce *or* | _____ | _____ |
|     Gravy | _____ | _____ |
|   Pork & Beans *or* | _____ | _____ |
|     Vegetarian Beans | _____ | _____ |
|   Beans (Pinto, Kidney | _____ | _____ |
|     Chick Peas, etc.) | _____ | _____ |
|   Peanut Butter | _____ | _____ |
| | | |
| *Vegetables* | | |
|   Cans | _____ | _____ |
|   Potatoes *or* Yams | _____ | _____ |
| | | |
| *Fruit* | | |
|   Juice | _____ | _____ |
|   Cans | _____ | _____ |
|   Jelly | _____ | _____ |
| | | |
| *Bread* | | |
|   Rice *or* Barley | _____ | _____ |
|   Macaroni & Cheese | _____ | _____ |
|   Cereal *or* Pancake Mix & Syrup | _____ | _____ |
|   Crackers *or* Muffins *or* Biscuit Mix | _____ | _____ |
| | | |
| *Soup* | | |
|   Canned *or* Dry | _____ | _____ |

*(other categories—over)*

| CATEGORY | AMOUNT | COMMENTS |
|----------|--------|----------|

*Baby*
   Baby Cereal
   Baby Food
   Baby Formula
   Baby Juice

*Extras that May Be Considered:*

*Condiments/Misc.*
   Catsup
   Flour
   Honey
   Mayonnaise
   Mustard
   Pepper
   Pickles
   Relish
   Salad Dressing
   Salt
   Seasonings
   Shortening
   Sugar
   Vegetable Oil
   Vinegar

*Desserts*
   Jello
   Pudding

*Drinks*
   Coffee
   Hot Cocoa
   Tea

# OUTREACH
# FOOD PROGRAM
## *Distribution Form*

Everyone is entitled to basic foods

| CATEGORY | DATE: | DATE: | DATE: | DATE: |
|---|---|---|---|---|
| *Milk* | | | | |
| Powdered | —— | —— | —— | —— |
| Evaporated/Condensed | —— | —— | —— | —— |
| | | | | |
| *Meat/Protein* | | | | |
| Cans—Meat | —— | —— | —— | —— |
| Cans—Fish | —— | —— | —— | —— |
| Pasta/Noodles with | —— | —— | —— | —— |
| Spaghetti Sauce *or* | —— | —— | —— | —— |
| Tomato Sauce *or* | —— | —— | —— | —— |
| Gravy | —— | —— | —— | —— |
| Pork & Beans *or* | —— | —— | —— | —— |
| Vegetarian Beans | —— | —— | —— | —— |
| Beans (Pinto, Kidney | —— | —— | —— | —— |
| Chick Peas, etc.) | —— | —— | —— | —— |
| Peanut Butter | —— | —— | —— | —— |
| | | | | |
| *Vegetables* | | | | |
| Cans | —— | —— | —— | —— |
| Potatoes *or* Yams | —— | —— | —— | —— |
| | | | | |
| *Fruit* | | | | |
| Juice | —— | —— | —— | —— |
| Cans | —— | —— | —— | —— |
| Jelly | —— | —— | —— | —— |
| | | | | |
| *Bread* | | | | |
| Rice *or* Barley | —— | —— | —— | —— |
| Macaroni & Cheese | —— | —— | —— | —— |
| Cereal *or* Pancake Mix & Syrup | —— | —— | —— | —— |
| Crackers *or* Muffins *or* Biscuit Mix | —— | —— | —— | —— |
| | | | | |
| *Soup* | | | | |
| Canned *or* Dry | —— | —— | —— | —— |

*(other categories—over)*

| CATEGORY | DATE: | DATE: | DATE: | DATE: |
|---|---|---|---|---|
| *Baby* | | | | |
| Baby Cereal | ___ | ___ | ___ | ___ |
| Baby Food | ___ | ___ | ___ | ___ |
| Baby Formula | ___ | ___ | ___ | ___ |
| Baby Juice | ___ | ___ | ___ | ___ |
| | | | | |
| *Extras that May Be Considered:* | | | | |
| | | | | |
| *Condiments/Misc.* | | | | |
| Catsup | ___ | ___ | ___ | ___ |
| Flour | ___ | ___ | ___ | ___ |
| Honey | ___ | ___ | ___ | ___ |
| Mayonnaise | ___ | ___ | ___ | ___ |
| Mustard | ___ | ___ | ___ | ___ |
| Pepper | ___ | ___ | ___ | ___ |
| Pickles | ___ | ___ | ___ | ___ |
| Relish | ___ | ___ | ___ | ___ |
| Salad Dressing | ___ | ___ | ___ | ___ |
| Salt | ___ | ___ | ___ | ___ |
| Seasonings | ___ | ___ | ___ | ___ |
| Shortening | ___ | ___ | ___ | ___ |
| Sugar | ___ | ___ | ___ | ___ |
| Vegetable Oil | ___ | ___ | ___ | ___ |
| Vinegar | ___ | ___ | ___ | ___ |
| | | | | |
| *Desserts* | | | | |
| Jello | ___ | ___ | ___ | ___ |
| Pudding | ___ | ___ | ___ | ___ |
| | | | | |
| *Drinks* | | | | |
| Coffee | ___ | ___ | ___ | ___ |
| Hot Cocoa | ___ | ___ | ___ | ___ |
| Tea | ___ | ___ | ___ | ___ |

# OUTREACH
# FOOD PROGRAM
*Volunteer Preference Form*

Name_____     Date_____

Address _____     Telephone_____

_____

|  | *Morning Hours 8-12 Noon* | *Afternoon/Evening Hours 12-9 P.M.* |
|---|---|---|
| Monday | _____ | _____ |
| Tuesday | _____ | _____ |
| Wednesday | _____ | _____ |
| Thursday | _____ | _____ |
| Friday | _____ | _____ |
| Saturday | _____ | _____ |
| Sunday | _____ | _____ |

*Frequency:*     ____ Weekly     ____ Monthly     ____ When Needed     ____ Other

Comments:_____

_____

_____

_____

_____

_____

_____

Thank You!

# OUTREACH
## *Food Distribution Center–Monthly Schedule*

| Time | Week No. 1 | Week No. 2 | Week No. 3 | Week No. 4 | Week No. 5 |
|---|---|---|---|---|---|
| 3:00–4:00 | | | | | |
| 4:00–5:00 | | | | | |
| 5:00–6:00 | | | | | |
| 6:00–7:00 | | | | | |
| 7:00–8:00 | | | | | |

Please refer to the reverse side of this page to phone a substitute (odd week call even week, even week call odd week *in your own time slot*) in the event you are unable to make an assigned time. If there are any questions, please leave a message at the Outreach office. Also, please notify Outreach office *in advance* when you are not able to make an assigned time and let us know who will be your substitute. Thank you, and God bless.

# PHONE A SUBSTITUTE

| Volunteer | Phone | Volunteer | Phone |
|-----------|-------|-----------|-------|
|           |       |           |       |
|           |       |           |       |
|           |       |           |       |
|           |       |           |       |
|           |       |           |       |
|           |       |           |       |
|           |       |           |       |
|           |       |           |       |
|           |       |           |       |
|           |       |           |       |
|           |       |           |       |
|           |       |           |       |

# OUTREACH
# FOOD PROGRAM
## *Hot Meals Assessment Guide*

Name_____ Telephone_____

Address _____

## *Assessment*

Date _____

*Consistency:*      *Has:*                    *Food Preferences:*

   Regular____    Microwave ____    _____

   Soft    ____    Oven     ____    _____

   Puree  ____    Neither  ____    _____

                                   _____

*Allergies:*        *Can Reheat*             _____

   Yes    ____    Yes   ____    _____

   No     ____    No    ____    _____

   _____                              _____

   _____                              _____

   _____                              _____

*Food Dislikes:*                            _____

_____                      _____

_____

_____

_____

_____         *Day of Meal*

_____         ____ Monday

_____         ____ Tuesday

_____         ____ Wednesday

_____         ____ Thursday

_____         ____ Friday

_____         *Approximate Delivery Time:* _____

Name: Volunteer Assessor _____    Phone _____

*(For additional comments, use other side)*

# Chapter 8
# Consciousness Raising

*Lord Jesus, through the goodness of your life and the service you provided people you were a witness of God's love for all creation. You helped sick and suffering people, curing the blind and the lame, raising the dead and proclaiming the good news to the poor. We draw upon your example, Jesus, and we ask that through you God will grant us the blessing to become the Christians we claim to be. May people find comfort and solace through our compassionate and accepting presence. Let us, too, proclaim the good news to all people through our loving service done in your name, Jesus Christ, our Lord. Amen.*

The aim of consciousness raising is to elicit a compassionate response from local community residents toward the needy neighbor.

Sensitizing an individual Christian or a community of Christians to a neighbor's less fortunate circumstance or need generally evokes an inner response, which thoughts may be logical or along problem solving lines. An individual's/community's thoughts will be rooted in their own experiences, beliefs and attitudes. The needs of their neighbor can challenge the individual/community about personal and collective thoughts, beliefs and behaviors. Powerful impressions can result within the thinker/thinking community effecting movement and growth. Resultant attitudinal changes can benefit the neighbor in need.

The object of consciousness raising is to evoke individual reflection and suggest proposals for action. Consciousness raising techniques can be uncomplicated, direct and simple. Examples follow and include:

1. announcements—for immediate attention and action
2. weekly bulletin—for reflection, information sharing, and action
3. Prayer of the Faithful—for communal awareness and reflection
4. public witness/high visibility efforts—for communal attention and/or issue emphasis.

## Announcements

The simple announcement (delivered at Sunday liturgies) which follows allows the reader actual feedback relative to the impressions made on individual listeners. Note the varied responses of individuals in the congregation indicative of movement and growth. The positive momentum reverberates within the community, calling some to action.

The announcement for reflection (consciousness raising) was

A married couple with two small children ages 15 months and 8 years has asked help from Outreach. The mother has had a recurrence of cancer and will enter the hospital this week during which time the husband will take off from work to care for the children. After discharge the mother will need assistance lifting and caring, especially for her baby. If you can help or for further information call the Outreach office. Thank you.

received at the liturgies in absolute silence and in an unusual stillness. The following day two women in the parish offered to assist this family. The two women who volunteered had two young children of their own and were able to easily identify with the mother in need. The volunteer women expressed deep compassion which they admitted compelled them to action. Within a week's time a third woman volunteered her assistance. This third woman volunteer was a registered nurse, never married, who had cared for her suffering middle-aged mother who eventually died of cancer. Within that week there also followed many individuals who expressed concern for the family in need. There was talk of real desire to assist this family but regret at not being able to help at this time. Expressions of sadness, concern and wanting to help could be heard from people who, like the three volunteer women, identified closely with this family as to age, number of children, or with the illness itself. Women said they thanked God for their own health and could not imagine the uncertainty and pain this woman must be experiencing.

Christian consciousness raising especially about issues close to home impact upon those made aware. Individuals, families, and communities can experience attitudinal and behavioral changes following the consciousness raising challenge of reflective thinking. Action (donating money, food, clothing, or other items, volunteerism) rebounds from healthy self-awareness which identifies us all as brothers and sisters.

## Using the Bulletin for Information/Sharing

In addition to announcements at liturgies, the weekly bulletin can be used to inform and foster thinking among the local residents.

*Example A*

---

### HOMELESS PERSONS

Over the last four months, homeless men and women have presented themselves to Outreach for assistance. Because problems of the homeless are urgent and as varied as are their personalities and the degree of their well-being or ill-being, Outreach has had to be flexible, creative, patient and persistent in assisting the multifaceted basic life crises of the homeless individual. For the next couple of weeks, this little column will highlight the types of homeless people who reside in our neighborhood.

Outreach ministers to anyone who presents himself or herself at our door, including the homeless. Six homeless individuals living near the church have come to Outreach seeking help. While none of these six men and women were locally born or raised, all now have either relatives or friends who live here. These homeless persons feel, therefore, that here is "home" and they have some sense of community and of caring. For various and complex reasons, however, these people are unable even to live with the very people to whom they are tied by blood or friendship. They remain without a place to call home.

Sometimes addictions of one kind or another (alcohol, drugs, sex, gambling) contribute to people not having a place to stay. Some suffer from depression such as caused by job loss or the death or illness of family members. Often their own mental and/or physical health is not good. All homeless people experience emotional turmoil, feeling rejected, perhaps blaming themselves to the point of self-hate.

The first step for Outreach is to be open to the needs of our homeless neighbors. Through openness, caring and listening, the pain is heard and issues can be addressed. The process is slow, but eventually through consistent listening, caring and advising, some homeless people can be helped to help themselves. (Next week: Where do local homeless people reside?)

---

## HOMELESS PERSONS (Continued):
## WHERE DO THE LOCAL HOMELESS RESIDE?

The six homeless individuals who live in our area and who have come to Outreach for assistance live in various spaces in our neighborhood. While they walk in the vicinity during the day, they sleep in various places. Sometimes they inhabit the benches in "Triangle Park" on Jamaica Avenue. Some sleep under the platform of the train station off of the boulevard. There is an abandoned gas station farther down the avenue to the east where people "camp out at night," and two of the six often sleep in abandoned cars.

Homeless people lead a nomadic existence. They are a living reminder that all of us are in search of our everlasting home. We will be restless until we rest in God. (Next week: How does Outreach assist the area's homeless?)

## HOMELESS PERSONS (Continued):
## HOW DOES OUTREACH ASSIST THE AREA'S HOMELESS?

Perhaps this question can be most clearly answered by a short case story. (Names have been omitted; the story is true.)

Mr. X came to Outreach stating that he lost his job as a gas station attendant one month ago. He is 36 years old and had been renting an apartment in our neighborhood. Because of the lack of income resulting from his job loss, Mr. X was unable to make his rent payment and subsequently lost his apartment. Mr. X has been living in the street and sleeping in the park on Jamaica Ave. for one week. He has been hungry and survives by picking the garbage and by stealing fruit from the fruit stands along the avenue. He has been searching for a job but feels that he is growing more dirty and offensive each day because he has nowhere to groom himself and no change of clothing. Mr. X appears depressed and discouraged. He came to Outreach on the recommendation of a "man in a car who passes by the park each morning and who told me to go to Outreach for help."

After his interview, Mr. X received immediate food from our Outreach pantry. He was also provided with soap and a referral was made for him to receive clothing from another nearby church. Next, Mr. X and I worked out a plan for a mailing address for Mr. X so he could immediately apply for emergency public assistance (so he could pay rent until he got a job), Medicaid, and food stamps. I sent Mr. X off with a letter to expedite this financial assistance, and another appointment was made for Mr. X to return to Outreach to talk about housing. (More about Mr. X next week).

## HOMELESS PERSONS (MR. X Continued)

On his first visit to Outreach Mr. X's need for food, clothing, and hygiene were addressed. Initial steps were taken to improve his financial status. When Mr. X returned to Outreach for the second time, he had followed through on all the recommendations of his previous visit to Outreach. Seeing Mr. X's sincerity and potential, Outreach called upon St. Vincent de Paul's financial assistance which paid for Mr. X to stay one week at a local YMCA. At the Y Mr. X would have some place to care for his hygiene. The Y would also give Mr. X the security of keeping several personal possessions.

Example A approaches consciousness raising through a series of "bulletin blurbs" citing perhaps the shocking reality of homelessness in the neighborhood. After sensitizing the parish to this local phenomenon, the consciousness raising intent (to arouse compassion in those made aware) is to explore factors which affect homelessness and afflict homeless persons. Mr. X is a real person and is presented to community residents in an effort to help them admit the reality of homelessness in the neighborhood, to further the understanding of the circumstances contributing to homelessness, and to work toward Christian acceptance of people regardless of their situation.

*Example B*

---

### AIDS AWARENESS

AIDS Awareness at our parish began months ago when I received the first call for a young AIDS mother and her baby boy. I began then to write a short "article" each week for our Outreach column because I thought that many people believed that AIDS is "out there," that AIDS is not here in my home and that AIDS is not in our parish family. After our AIDS awareness workshop given in our parish by experts and specialists in the field of AIDS some people still say "Who us? AIDS? Never!"

Well, AIDS is here among our own. I've been to visit the home of this young mother I speak about. She has AIDS and so does her baby. They live nearby and are members of our parish family (there are others). This young mother tells me that when she was first diagnosed, she had great fear of what would happen to her physically. Now she says she suffers more from being isolated and rejected even by members of her own family. She says she has concern that people no longer visit her or will have a meal at her house. She spends all of her time at home with her baby, and because she is unable to get help from any other sector, she has had to rely on the gay men's society to assist her with household chores and shopping. She finds this arrangement very uncomfortable but necessary. What she needs now is someone to watch her baby once a week for a couple of hours.

I ask you the readers and supporters of our parish Outreach to search your hearts. I am not asking you right now to volunteer to watch this baby. I am simply asking you to put yourself before God in an attitude of prayer. Ask God to bless our parish family (that means you and me, too) with God-like understanding and compassion. Beg the Holy Spirit to give us the courage to want to know the truth about AIDS and about ourselves. I ask you to please pray over the scriptures and learn how Jesus responded to the "unacceptable" people of his time—the woman caught in adultery, the lepers, sinners, tax collectors, the sick, the insane—and ask Jesus to make our hearts like his.

---

Example B, on the other hand, reflects a persistent approach to consciousness raising about AIDS, an issue firmly and consistently denied by the local community. The strategy demonstrated by this example is to reinforce information already raised in previous bulletin series and an educational workshop sponsored by the parish on the topic of AIDS and to begin to prepare people for an invitation to a gathering for further information, input and group sharing. This two edged approach is strong and when selectively used can help soften the defenses and persistent denial of people and congregations to a shocking reality.

### The Prayer of the Faithful

The liturgy's Prayer of the Faithful can also be used to raise consciousness. Examples of intercessions are given on the following page. Note that consciousness raising can sometimes be subtle and closely aligned with volunteer recruitment.

### Public Witness/High Visibility

Food is a basic human need which no one can deny and with which all people can identify. Consciousness raising relative to hunger and/or local food needs, therefore, can have a high impact upon the community. The following paragraphs explain how to conduct, cooperatively organize and publicly execute a consciousness raising program through simple and effective hunger awareness efforts. Important initial ground rules will be explained in the following pages. They include:
1. using consciousness raising where poverty and hunger would likely be less obvious and where the community's denial will most probably be the strongest
2. keeping consciousness raising efforts simple
3. readying simple flyers or handouts for distribution (see samples on pages 115–120).

Note the geographical location of your parish in relation to the larger supermarket chains. All of these food stores attract their own clientele. There may be the tendency for the "middle class population" or perhaps a specific ethnic group to frequent one particular food store while different ethnic or economic clientele may select another place for regular food purchases. In keeping with ground rule #1, select the location and learn the name of the store manager. Introduce yourself to the manager by visiting the

# PRAYER OF THE FAITHFUL: SAMPLE INTERCESSIONS

- For women who suffer from a poor self image, for prostitutes and drug abusers, especially for those who have sought assistance through our parish's Outreach that through our loving acceptance they may begin to be healed and be part of our family . . .

- For victims of violence, especially those in our own parish community, for abused and used people of all nationalities and ages, that through our loving attention and prayers they may be able to forgive and seek assistance . . .

- For God's blessings upon all those in our parish who suffer debilitating illnesses such as Alzheimer's and Parkinson's disease and for our Outreach volunteers who assist them in their homes . . .

- For the unemployed and the underpaid, for those who struggle to feed, clothe and house themselves and their families, that our parish's Outreach efforts and our prayers may bolster their courage and assist them in their search for justice . . .

- For those who suffer humiliation and shame because of the systemic injustices of our social systems, that the public witness of our Outreach efforts and the support of our parish family may strengthen them and be hope for them . . .

- That those who come to Outreach pregnant and troubled may find in us acceptance, support and concrete Christian assistance which encourages hope and life . . .

- For children of single parents who often must assume an adult role in the family, that through our prayers and Outreach efforts we may help to free them for childhood by ministering to the family as a unit . . .

- For those who are experiencing a mid-life crisis, that God may strengthen them and that through their patient endurance they may arrive at new strength and wholeness . . .

- For single parents who feel unsupported in their struggle to raise their children, that they may be open to the care and friendship of others . . .

- For all those in our neighborhood who are at risk for homelessness, especially for the elderly and single parent mothers, that homeowners will be considerate and just in their rent practices . . .

- That through the kindness and love of our Outreach volunteers, God will be strength and hope for those adults and children in our parish who suffer with AIDS . . .

store, telling him about the Outreach program's purpose of helping people in need of food and basic necessities. Convey that the goals of the separate "businesses" would be furthered through joint cooperation because the expected outcome will be increased food purchases at his store as exiting buyers donate food stuffs to the Outreach program.

Regardless of the manager's initial response, formalize the request in a letter addressed to the manager (see sample below). Include the projected dates for this hunger awareness implementation. Sometimes managers must present such a letter to the supervisor of the store before final permission is given. Generally, managers and supervisors welcome the idea of non-intrusive and pleasant neighborhood people greeting buyers at their supermarket entrances. It is good public relations as well as good business for them.

---

### SAMPLE LETTER TO MANAGER

Mr./Ms._____ , Manager

Address _____

Dear Mr./Ms. _____:

    I send thanks your way for the assistance you give to neighborhood people. In some ways we are in the same business, that of helping people.

    Our church's Outreach program aims to provide people with needed food. In order to maintain and upgrade our program, Outreach wants to heighten the community's awareness of the hungry in our neighborhood. Accordingly, we have designed a simple approach which we believe will mutually assist you and Outreach.

    The hunger awareness weekend we propose consists of Outreach volunteers standing at a table by the store entrances. An informational flyer relative to hunger and our program's response to this need would be distributed by the volunteers.

    Our church would publicize the event in the weekly parish bulletin, asking families to help support Outreach's hunger awareness efforts by shopping at your store. We anticipate that buyers will support our efforts by increased spending at your store so they can donate some food item(s) to the Outreach program.

    Should you be interested and agree to this mutually beneficial plan, the weekend of Friday October_____ through Sunday October_____ seems ideal for us.

    Our parish Outreach Program awaits your response and we thank you for considering a hunger awareness weekend at your store.

Sincerely,

Outreach Director

---

Once permission is received, sequentially place a variety of blurbs in the weekly bulletin. This will attract people interested in helping. Observe ground rule #2 by keeping the requests simple. Be very specific about the *limited* time donation of a volunteer.

---

SAMPLE BULLETIN BLURBS

Hunger Awareness: Remember the hungry of our neighborhood! Outreach volunteers will be needed to help raise neighborhood awareness and food donating at
_____ (supermarket name)
on _____ (dates)
Tell Your Neighbors!

Hunger Awareness: Yes! _____ (name of supermarket and address)
will host our hunger awareness weekend on _____ (date).
One hour is all it takes—and most volunteers anticipate it will be "fun."
Volunteer and find out! Call Outreach. Thanks.

Hunger Awareness: The presence of volunteers at
_____(supermarket name)
at_____(address)
on_____(dates)
will be testimony to the care and concern we have for the hungry in our neighborhood.
Mark your calendars! New volunteers are welcome. Call Outreach. Thank you.

---

Flyers can be used to attract hunger awareness volunteers (see page 112). These can be distributed as inserts in the weekly bulletin or they can be left at church entrances.

Next invite all potential volunteers to an open and optional informational meeting. Use the bulletin (see below) and the pulpit to call forth volunteers.

---

INVITATION IN BULLETIN

Hunger Awareness:
All those who wish to assist our hunger awareness weekend on _____ should come to an informational meeting Wednesday _____ at ____P.M. in the rectory. Thank you.

---

# OUTREACH

## HUNGER AWARENESS — FOOD RAISING

At _____ Supermarket

on _____ Avenue

Will you help make our village residents aware of the poverty and hunger that exist in our neighborhood?

We need your presence at the doors of _____ Supermarket.

---

I am interested in giving some time to the Food Pantry Project.

| Schedule me for _____ hour(s) for the time(s) below. | |
|---|---|
| Friday, April 20 (8:00 AM – 9:00 PM) | Hour(s) FROM        TO |
| Saturday, April 21 (8:00 AM – 7:00 PM) | FROM        TO |
| Sunday, April 22 (9:00 AM – 5:00 PM) | FROM        TO |

Name _____        Phone _____

### PLEASE RETURN FORM TO THE RECTORY — THANK YOU!

---

Outreach will attempt to schedule the hour(s) according to your stated preference.

We will phone you to confirm the requested time.

You will receive an "orientation" when you arrive at the supermarket.

If you would like more information before volunteering,

call Outreach at (phone) _____.

This informational gathering is the time for articulating the goals of the awareness project. Provide paper and pencil for volunteers to indicate the one-hour time block donation they wish to give. Remind them that their purpose is to be present in groups of two outside the supermarket where they will speak to people and hand out Outreach information (ground rule #3). Be sure to have a copy of the hunger awareness volunteer schedule (see sample, page 121) at each door so that volunteers can welcome their replacements by name. Two volunteers should be posted at each of the store entrances, with a small card table at each entrance for the maintenance of Outreach literature and to receive any food donations.

Annual or bi-annual (spring and fall) hunger awareness weekends prove effective. Upon completion of each weekend, share the impressions of the project with the store manager by way of a letter of thanks:

---

### SAMPLE LETTER OF THANKS

Mr./Ms._____, Manager
_____Supermarket
Address _____

Dear Mr./Ms. _____ :
   Thanks to you, Parish Outreach conducted a successful hunger awareness and food raising project at your store the weekend of _____. The goal of heightening people's awareness of hungry neighbors and receiving donations of food for Outreach's food program were well met.
   We thank you and your staff for your spirit of cooperation and for your interest. We trust the weekend was equally beneficial to your aims also.
   God's blessings upon the good we endeavor to do through our respective jobs!

Sincerely,


Outreach Director

---

The parish bulletin can be used to share impressions with and express gratitude to the people of the parish:

SAMPLE BULLETIN THANKS

Hunger Awareness/Thanks
Sincerest thanks and congratulations to all! Great applause for your excellent service! Our
Hunger Awareness efforts at _____ were a great success. Outreach's presence was a testimony to the care and concern we have for the hungry in our neighborhood
and to the generosity of all those who helped.
    Many shoppers contributed canned and boxed food items so that our Food Distribution
shelves are proud and full. During this weekend, we also received $155.00 in money dona-
tions. Thank you, one and all!

Note that the samples are sure to applaud all volunteers as well as
food donors for their witness to neighborhood concerns. Simple
thanks can also be expressed in prayers of the liturgy:

We pray in thanksgiving to God for all of you who serve our neighborhood's needy
through Outreach and for the success of our hunger awareness efforts. Let us pray to the
Lord.

Hunger awareness weekends are generally successful. Long
after the weekends pass, expect
1. to receive calls from shoppers wishing to refer people in
   need;
2. that people will want to donate food regularly to the program;
3. that some shoppers will have joined the Outreach program as
   volunteers;
4. increased cooperation with food chains who are happy for
   the increased spending and pleasantry at their store.
    The aim of consciousness raising is to elicit a compassionate
response from people by raising individuals' awareness of suffering people among their own family members and within the local
community. Sensitizing the Christian community and the community at large through well organized, timely, repetitive and rhyth-
mic awareness approaches can impact upon people's sensitivities,
attitudes and behaviors. Consciousness raising can give birth to
caring people and caring communities.

# Our Lady of Lourdes

O
U
T
R
E
A
C
H

**FOR
QUEENS VILLAGE
PEOPLE**

*Front*

Our Lady of Lourdes Church
92-96 220th Street
Queens Village, N.Y 11428

479-5111

*Back*

OUTREACH

A Program for People Who Live in Queens Village

Outreach at Our Lady of Lourdes began in September 1985 with a small group of volunteers serving the sick of Queens Village in their homes. As the needs of the sick and their families became known, Our Lady of Lourdes began to reach out to other area needs. Basic life-support programs developed through Outreach to address people's legitimate needs for food, clothing, shelter, employment, care of single-parent children and financial aid.

In less than a year, the scope of the work significantly enlarged. Awareness of local needs drew other church leaders together in a strong cooperative spirit. This Ecumenical spirit remains supportive of the endeavors of Our Lady of Lourdes Outreach which reaches out, without discrimination, to assist the area's poor. In the spirit of the gospel, area churches endeavor to reflect "their neighbor's" needs to the local community and to elicit a compassionate response.

Through Outreach, 720 people from Queens Village—professional and non-professional, men and women, teens and adults—have volunteered to assist the needy. Over 204 area families with sick member(s) have benefited from the volunteer assistance (personal care, shopping, housecleaning, meal preparation) of Our Lady of Lourdes Outreach. Our Food Program provides 8,667 meals annually and offers neighborhood people other basic care. For some, there have been successful outcomes for employment and housing. Over 800 bereaved families have been touched by us. In cooperation with public and private agencies, Outreach serves hundreds of the neighborhood's needy.

For those in Queens Village who present themselves in legitimate need, Outreach extends a "Welcome!" Outreach is people caring for people in response to the neighbor in need. Outreach is the love commandment made visible—Love your neighbor as yourself. "And who is the neighbor? The one who treats another with compassion."

*Inside*

116

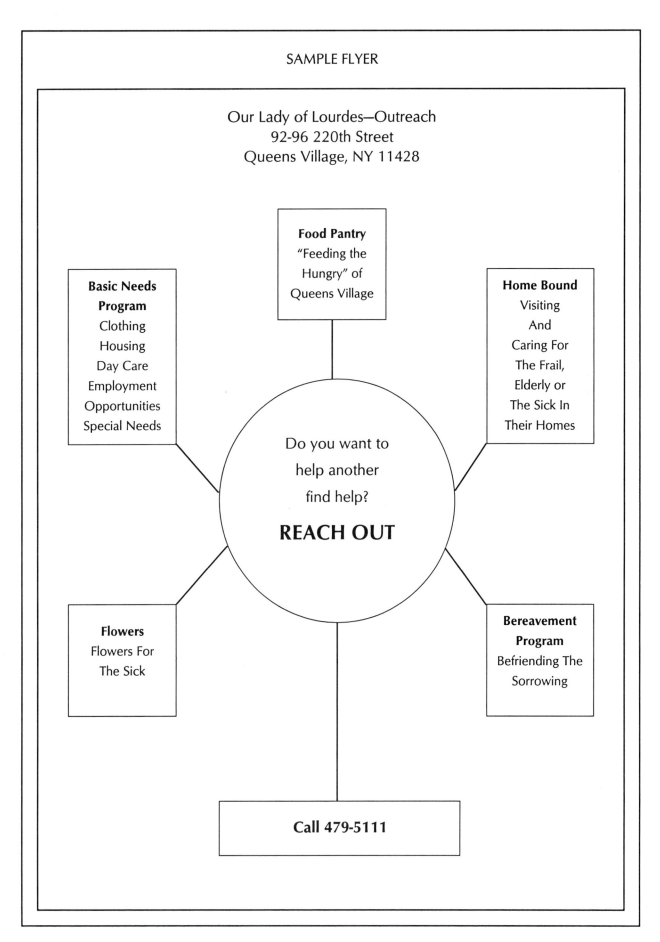

Our Lady of Lourdes—Outreach
92-96 220th Street
Queens Village, NY 11428

**Food Pantry**
"Feeding the
Hungry" of
Queens Village

**Basic Needs
Program**
Clothing
Housing
Day Care
Employment
Opportunities
Special Needs

**Home Bound**
Visiting
And
Caring For
The Frail,
Elderly or
The Sick In
Their Homes

Do you want to
help another
find help?

**REACH OUT**

**Flowers**
Flowers For
The Sick

**Bereavement
Program**
Befriending The
Sorrowing

**Call 479-5111**

Our Lady of Lourdes Church
92-96 220th Street
Queens Village, New York 11428

# OUTREACH

People in need who live in Queens Village can find help at Our Lady of Lourdes Church.

Our Lady of Lourdes Outreach program assists the area's hungry with food items donated by area residents.

If you know someone who needs food—
 call Outreach—479-5111

If you would like to help us serve the needs of the hungry in our neighborhood, please—
 consider even a small donation of food
 and/or
 call 479-5111 to find out how you can help!

La Iglesia de Nuestra Señora de Lourdes quiere ayudar a la gente que vive en Queens Village y que necessita ayuda de comida o ropa.

Si alguna persona sabe de alguien que necessita comida o ropa—
 llamen a 479-5111.

THANK YOU!
Sr. Nancy Vendura
Director of Outreach

## LA IGLESIA NECESITA (POR FAVOR)

### LATAS DE

| | |
|---|---|
| Jugo | Frijoles ojinegros |
| Carne | Betabeles |
| Picadillo | Zanahorias |
| Espaquettes y | Maiz |
| Albondiga | Frijoles verdes |
| Salsa de tomate | Habas |
| Atún | Guisantes |
| Frutas | Guisantes/zanahorias |
| Tomates | Patatas |
| Sopa | Espinaca |

### PAQUETES DE ALIMENTOS

| | |
|---|---|
| Cereal (caliente/frio) | |
| Budin/marmelada | Patatas instantes |
| Leche instante | Macarrones y queso |
| Galletas | Tortita de harina/sirup |

### MISCELANEO

| | |
|---|---|
| Café | Compota de manzana |
| Cacao | Jaleas |
| Té | Mantequilla de cacahuate |
| Azúcar | Maronesa |

## OUR FOOD PROGRAM NEEDS ARE:

### CANNED GOODS

| | |
|---|---|
| Juices | Baked Beans |
| Meats | Beets |
| Hash | Carrots |
| Meatballs/Spaghetti | Corn |
| Spam | Green Beans |
| Stew | Lima Beans |
| Ravioli | Peas |
| Tomato Sauce | Peas/Carrots |
| Tuna Fish | Potatoes |
| Fruits | Spinach |
| Soups | Tomatoes |
| | Wax Beans |

### PACKAGED GOODS

| | |
|---|---|
| Cereal (Hot/Cold) | |
| Jello/Pudding | Instant Potatoes |
| Milk (Instant) | Macaroni & Cheese |
| Rice | Pancake Mix/Syrup |
| | Saltines |

### MISCELLANEOUS

| | |
|---|---|
| Coffee | Apple Sauce |
| Cocoa | Jelly/Jams |
| Tea Bags | Peanut Butter |
| Sugar | Mayonnaise |

# OUTREACH
## *Hunger Awareness Schedule*

| | | Front Door | | Rear Door |
|---|---|---|---|---|
| 8 – 9 | 1 | | 3 | |
| | 2 | | 4 | |
| 9 – 10 | 1 | | 3 | |
| | 2 | | 4 | |
| 11 – 12 | 1 | | 3 | |
| | 2 | | 4 | |
| 12 – 1 | 1 | | 3 | |
| | 2 | | 4 | |
| 1 – 2 | 1 | | 3 | |
| | 2 | | 4 | |
| 2 – 3 | 1 | | 3 | |
| | 2 | | 4 | |
| 3 – 4 | 1 | | 3 | |
| | 2 | | 4 | |
| 4 – 5 | 1 | | 3 | |
| | 2 | | 4 | |
| 5 – 6 | 1 | | 3 | |
| | 2 | | 4 | |
| 6 – 7 | 1 | | 3 | |
| | 2 | | 4 | |

*IF A NO SHOW, CALL OUTREACH.*

# Chapter 9
# Employment, Child Care, and Shelter Programs

*O God, we pray for people who are finding life difficult, people who are wanting and needing others to help them obtain employment, shelter or the care of their children. Couple our prayers and our good works with those of the people of our parish. Bless the searching people who call us for help in their time of need. Through our facilitation help them to find someone who will be sensitive and caring. We ask you also, our loving God, to bless potential good Samaritans who have the personal and material resources to help others in need. Inspire and empower a compassionate response in them so that they will gladly share their gifts and their time with others. We ask this in Jesus' name. Amen.*

While the population and the goals of people needing employment, child care and/or shelter assistance differ, program planning and implementation methods are very similar.

Because these particular programs generally attract telephone callers rather than personal contacts between people needing services (recipients) and those offering them (volunteers), the employment, shelter and child care programs are greatly dependent upon organized records and recording tools which will facilitate the necessary mediation and negotiation. Each program requires two forms and two files or binders—one which documents "recipient information" (recipient form) and one which records the potential volunteer (volunteer form). Unlike all the other Outreach programs, these three programs do not require a face to face interview with the potential volunteer. As "broker," Outreach's true contribution is to connect the recipient with the potential volunteer and educate both sides to screen and choose who is mutually suitable.

The usage and procedure of both forms for each program is styled on Outreach as the broker. When a caller or visitor requests a need for employment and/or child care and/or shelter, all information is recorded on the recipient form. Similarly, the volunteer form is used to document information concerning people or businesses indicating the desire to assist someone in need. With this information so organized and available, the "matching" of needs against volunteer preferences and/or resources is relatively easy. The person requesting assistance is given one or more referrals with whom he or she makes direct contact. Remember to leave the screening and the selection to the participating persons. The reverse side of each form is used by the Outreach director to record all referrals and outcomes. Discussion and samples of these helpful instruments follow.

The Employment Program aims to assist the underemployed and the unemployed to find suitable work. The following record keeping tools can be helpful for successfully searching for and matching recipients and volunteers.

The employment program recipient form (see sample, pages 127–128) suggests documenting the date, name, address, and phone number of the person requesting employment. The front side of the form specifically clarifies the precise employment preference of the person in need. The reverse side of this recipient form, on the other hand, provides space for documenting outcomes and comments for each employment referral.

The employment program volunteer form (see sample, pages 129–130) records information about the business/employer volunteering to interview and possibly hire an unemployed person. The front side of this form includes the name of a contact person, possible job opportunities, and a description of the employment opening. Space for documenting outcome and comments for each employment referral is on the reverse side of the employment program volunteer form.

The Child Care Program aims to encourage opportunities for emotional respite, employment and financial independence for single mothers by negotiating safe child care at no or low cost. Two record keeping tools can be utilized to facilitate negotiations between single parents and willing child attenders.

The child care recipient form (see sample, pages 131–132) provides for a listing of the children needing to be cared for as well as a description of their sex and age, the hours of care needed and whether or not the mother can offer any payment for the services. An important recording on the form's front side is the mother's comments, which would include the special needs of any of her children (e.g. allergies to animals or edibles, food preferences, child's temperament, needs for rest, toileting, etc.).

The reverse side of this recipient form records the name of the volunteers to whom referral is made, the date of referral, and whether or not the mother accepted the referred volunteer. Room for the mother's or Outreach comments is also available.

The front side of the child care volunteer form (see sample, pages 133–134) includes the volunteer's preferences and attitudes regarding personal likes and dislikes about child caring responsibilities. A volunteer, for example, may be more inclined toward children of a particular sex or age. He or she may choose to engage in indoor activities rather than going for walks outdoors or playing in the park. Knowledge of child care volunteer attitudes and preferences is very important for assuring safe qualitative child care.

Like the reverse side of the employment and shelter volunteer form, the child care volunteer form provides space for documenting the outcome and comments for each child care referral.

The Shelter Program aims to assist the homeless and people at high risk for homelessness by helping them to find suitable housing. The following support the program's goal:

The shelter program recipient form (see sample, pages 135–136) allows for the documentation of the number of rooms needed by the homeless or the person/family at high risk. Included are the monthly rent expectations and the description of the searcher's likes or dislikes relative to housing.

The reverse side of the same form provides for the name of the contact person offering rentable space, the date of the referral and the outcome of the "match."

The front side of the shelter program volunteer form (see

sample, pages 137–138) records similar information but from the volunteer's point of view as opposed to or perhaps in conjunction with the recipient's perspective. Like expectations make potentially successful referrals or "matches." This form also allows for details about the available space being offered.

Information recorded on the reverse side of this volunteer form includes the name of the persons having need for shelter, the date, and the outcome of the referral.

While generally small, these Outreach programs can successfully assist people needing employment, respite, and shelter. In conjunction with the good Samaritan gospel story, willing people offer their service to others in time of need. Thus the unemployed or underemployed can be helped by local businesses (florists, car dealers, banks, dentists and doctors, etc.) who through Outreach have become aware of area residents needing work.

Single parents can profit by the brokerage of Outreach's recruiting, telephoning, screening and linking perspective volunteers with people needing no- or low-cost child care.

People with housing problems will doubtlessly remain the biggest challenge to an Outreach program. However, despite the neighborhood's insufficient dwellings, apartments, or housing units to meet the needs of people, Outreach can be successful in arranging shelter for some families by acting as liaison and negotiating between the volunteer and the family/persons in need.

These three programs will lend themselves well to the easy methodology of good record keeping coupled with the Christian theme of love and service to the needy neighbor.

# OUTREACH
## EMPLOYMENT PROGRAM
*Recipient Form*

Name_____     Date_____

Address _____     Telephone_____

_____

*Employment Preference:*

____ Office Work          ____ Housekeeping          ____ Maintenance

____ Typing               ____ Sales Person          ____ Other

*Description:* _____

_____

_____

_____

_____

_____

*Office Comments:* _____

_____

_____

_____

_____

_____

# EMPLOYMENT PROGRAM
### *Recipient Form*

| Date | Referral | Accepted | Comments |
|------|----------|----------|----------|
| | | | |
| | | | |
| | | | |
| | | | |
| | | | |
| | | | |
| | | | |
| | | | |
| | | | |
| | | | |
| | | | |
| | | | |
| | | | |
| | | | |
| | | | |
| | | | |

# OUTREACH
# EMPLOYMENT PROGRAM
## *Volunteer Form*

Name of Contact Person _____ Date_____

Phone Number of Contact Person _____

Name of Work Place _____

Address _____ Telephone_____

_____

*Type of Employment:*

_____ Office Work      _____ Housekeeping      _____ Maintenance

_____ Typing      _____ Sales Person      _____ Other

*Description:* _____

_____

_____

_____

_____

*Office Comments:* _____

_____

_____

_____

_____

# EMPLOYMENT PROGRAM
*Volunteer Form*

| Date | Person Referred | Accepted | Comments |
|------|-----------------|----------|----------|
| _____ | _____ | _____ | _____ |
| _____ | _____ | _____ | _____ |
| _____ | _____ | _____ | _____ |
| _____ | _____ | _____ | _____ |
| _____ | _____ | _____ | _____ |
| _____ | _____ | _____ | _____ |
| _____ | _____ | _____ | _____ |
| _____ | _____ | _____ | _____ |
| _____ | _____ | _____ | _____ |
| _____ | _____ | _____ | _____ |
| _____ | _____ | _____ | _____ |
| _____ | _____ | _____ | _____ |
| _____ | _____ | _____ | _____ |
| _____ | _____ | _____ | _____ |
| _____ | _____ | _____ | _____ |
| _____ | _____ | _____ | _____ |
| _____ | _____ | _____ | _____ |

# OUTREACH
## CHILD CARE PROGRAM
*Recipient Form*

Name_____     Date_____

Address _____     Telephone_____

_____

____ Single     ____ Married

*Children Needing Care:*

| | Name | Sex | Age |
|---|---|---|---|
| 1) | _____ | ___ | _____ |
| 2) | _____ | ___ | _____ |
| 3) | _____ | ___ | _____ |
| 4) | _____ | ___ | _____ |

*Hours of Caring Needed:* _____

*Ability to Pay:*     ____ per hour     ____ per week

*Mother's Comments:* _____

_____

_____

*Office Comments:* _____

_____

_____

_____

_____

# CHILD CARE
## Recipient Form

| Date | Volunteer | Accepted | Comments |
|------|-----------|----------|----------|
| | | | |
| | | | |
| | | | |
| | | | |
| | | | |
| | | | |
| | | | |
| | | | |
| | | | |
| | | | |
| | | | |
| | | | |
| | | | |
| | | | |
| | | | |
| | | | |

# OUTREACH
## CHILD CARE PROGRAM
### *Volunteer Form*

Name_____  Date_____

Address _____  Age _____

_____  Telephone_____

*Preference (Child)*                      *Hours Preferred*

____ 0 – Infant                            ____ A.M.

____ 2 – 3 Toddler                         ____ P.M.

____ 3 – 4 Pre-School

____ Young School Age                      *Donation per hour $_____*

____ Older School Age

*Likes:* _____          *Dislikes:* _____

_____                    _____

_____                    _____

_____                    _____

_____                    _____

*Office Comments:* _____

_____

_____

_____

_____

# CHILD CARE
*Volunteer Form*

| Date | Needs | Accepted | Comments |
|------|-------|----------|----------|
| _____ | _____ | _____ | _____ |
| _____ | _____ | _____ | _____ |
| _____ | _____ | _____ | _____ |
| _____ | _____ | _____ | _____ |
| _____ | _____ | _____ | _____ |
| _____ | _____ | _____ | _____ |
| _____ | _____ | _____ | _____ |
| _____ | _____ | _____ | _____ |
| _____ | _____ | _____ | _____ |
| _____ | _____ | _____ | _____ |
| _____ | _____ | _____ | _____ |
| _____ | _____ | _____ | _____ |
| _____ | _____ | _____ | _____ |
| _____ | _____ | _____ | _____ |
| _____ | _____ | _____ | _____ |
| _____ | _____ | _____ | _____ |
| _____ | _____ | _____ | _____ |

# OUTREACH
## SHELTER PROGRAM
*Recipient Form*

Name_____     Date_____

Address _____     Telephone_____

_____

*Rent Expectations:*     _____ per month

*Number of Rooms:*     _____

_____

_____

*Likes:* _____          *Dislikes:* _____

_____          _____

_____          _____

_____          _____

_____          _____

*Office Comments:* _____

_____

_____

_____

_____

_____

# SHELTER
*Recipient Form*

| Date | Referral | Accepted | Comments |
|------|----------|----------|----------|
| ____ | _____ | _____ | _____ |
| ____ | _____ | _____ | _____ |
| ____ | _____ | _____ | _____ |
| ____ | _____ | _____ | _____ |
| ____ | _____ | _____ | _____ |
| ____ | _____ | _____ | _____ |
| ____ | _____ | _____ | _____ |
| ____ | _____ | _____ | _____ |
| ____ | _____ | _____ | _____ |
| ____ | _____ | _____ | _____ |
| ____ | _____ | _____ | _____ |
| ____ | _____ | _____ | _____ |
| ____ | _____ | _____ | _____ |
| ____ | _____ | _____ | _____ |
| ____ | _____ | _____ | _____ |
| ____ | _____ | _____ | _____ |

# OUTREACH
## SHELTER PROGRAM
### *Volunteer Form*

Name_____ Date_____

Address _____ Telephone_____

_____

*Rent Expectations:* _____ per month

*Number of Rooms:* _____

*Description:* _____

_____

_____

*Likes:* _____    *Dislikes:* _____

_____    _____

_____    _____

_____    _____

_____    _____

*Office Comments:* _____

_____

_____

_____

_____

_____

# SHELTER
## *Volunteer Form*

| Date | Person Referred | Accepted | Comments |
|------|----------------|----------|----------|
| —— | ———— | —— | ————— |
| —— | ———— | —— | ————— |
| —— | ———— | —— | ————— |
| —— | ———— | —— | ————— |
| —— | ———— | —— | ————— |
| —— | ———— | —— | ————— |
| —— | ———— | —— | ————— |
| —— | ———— | —— | ————— |
| —— | ———— | —— | ————— |
| —— | ———— | —— | ————— |
| —— | ———— | —— | ————— |
| —— | ———— | —— | ————— |
| —— | ———— | —— | ————— |
| —— | ———— | —— | ————— |
| —— | ———— | —— | ————— |
| —— | ———— | —— | ————— |
| —— | ———— | —— | ————— |

# Chapter 10
# Prayer Corner

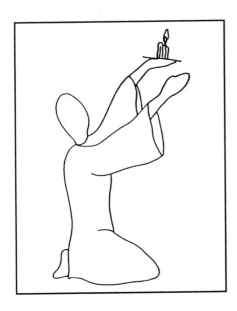

*Let our prayers rise like incense before you, O God, on behalf of all who enter our door. Bless them and love them through us, so that all may be strengthened on their life's journey. Through our ministry of prayer and compassionate action may people find here nourishment for body and spirit and peace of mind and heart. Inspired by your Holy Spirit we make this prayer to you, O God, united in Jesus' name. Amen.*

Outreach's prayer corner program is created out of the parish's desire to attract and spiritually support marginal people. Each of the parish Outreach programs discovers people of all faiths and needs and introduces them to a caring community who will call them by name and who will personally pray with them and for them.

Frequently the people who come to Outreach for assistance reveal that they experience feelings of disruption or alienation from God as a result of their suffering. They express not knowing how to vent their feelings toward God, thereby impeding their own healing and growth. "I want to pray to God," said one man, "but I just don't know how. Can you teach me?"

Some people consider one church as good as another. This perpetuates a sense of their not belonging anywhere, which further confirms their low self-esteem and the ultimate actual outcome that they are persons unknown by the church, uncared for, and perhaps unwanted even by God.

Troubled people may be secretly searching for the spiritual God of their journey. Poor self-image and emotions of embarrassment, shame, ignorance, or concern over appearance and/or behaviors may block people's search for God. The church itself with its formalized liturgy and sacramental structure can threaten people who can feel confronted and overwhelmed by an overly mature super-sophisticated, perhaps elegant-appearing Christianity.

The uncomplicated approach to the prayer corner by contrast with its personalized and gentle volunteer presence can powerfully symbolize the local church's welcome, warmth and care for all people.

The prayer corner is a quiet spot simply furnished. There may be a small table with a lit candle surrounded by a circle of chairs. Symbols and arrangements are unsophisticated and minimal so as not to be confusing or distracting to the purpose of prayer.

A manual of simple prayer services (see following samples) is a helpful guide for volunteers to use in assisting the prayer of people who visit the prayer corner. Themes of peace, God's love, and courage can be direct and relevant for the personal needs and style of this program's recipients. Devotional praying (scriptural rosary, for example) or according to the liturgical cycle (themes for Advent, Christmas, Lent, etc.) are other appropriate options which can be reflected in the prayer corner manual.

Begin by making the prayer corner available one day a week at peak time (the day of food distribution, for example). Put a large sign of welcome on the door of the prayer corner. This "sign" can take the form of a box labeled "Prayer Corner," which can also serve as a container for written petitions. All are welcome in the prayer corner. Individuals and families who come to receive food, can be invited to enter the prayer corner or submit a petition without obligation. The prayer corner offers people quiet space with opportunity to encounter a caring prayerful community (volunteers).

Here people are always "called by name." With great respect and gentleness all persons are accepted as they are and for who they are. Some people may choose to sit in silence. Others may state an intention for prayer. Some stand, others sit, some choose to kneel. Volunteers are flexible and alert to people and their prayer needs. They assist the spirit of prayer in silence, by spontaneous prayer or by sensitively using the prayer corner manual to pray with people or for people. Volunteers may help individuals find the words to speak their feelings and/or their needs to God. The petitions from the prayer box are always addressed by volunteers in the prayer corner program.

Through the kindness, gentleness, and acceptance by prayer corner volunteers, men, women, and children can discover personal growth, comfort and freedom of expression before their God whose compassion and love especially embraces the humble.

## PRAYER CORNER

### THEME: GOD'S LOVE (FOR CHILDREN)

LEADER:     Jesus loved the little children and wanted them near Him.

ALL:        Jesus loved the little children and wanted them near Him.

LEADER:     God, you loved us all so much that you sent us your own Son to come and live with us. He taught us many beautiful things about you: how much you love us and how you always forgive us when we do things that are wrong.

ALL:        Jesus loved the little children and wanted them near Him.

LEADER:     Whenever Jesus taught, people gathered around Him to listen. Often, there were so many people that Jesus got tired. But He always had time for the people He loved.

ALL:        Jesus loved the little children and wanted them near Him.

LEADER:     One time Jesus was so tired that He went off by Himself to rest. Some people saw Him, though, and sent their children over to Him so He could bless them. When Jesus' friends saw this they tried to stop them. "He's too tired," they said. But Jesus said, "No, let the children come. I am never too tired to listen to them."

ALL:        Jesus loved the little children and wanted them to be near Him.

LEADER:     Jesus, please help us to remember that you love all of us so much that you will always listen to us when we need to talk to you or if something is bothering us.

ALL:        Amen.

PRAYER CORNER

*THEME: PATIENCE*

OPENING HYMN

OPENING PRAYER   O God, you are the source of my life. In you I can find peace of mind and heart. Grant that I may accept the trials which come my way with patience and love and so imitate the life of Jesus your Son who lives with you and the Holy Spirit forever and ever. Amen.

PSALM   (All) O Lord, my God, I take refuge in you.

(Leader) O Lord, my God, in you I take refuge; save me from all my pursuers and rescue me, lest I become like the lion's prey, to be torn to pieces, with no one to rescue me.

(All) O Lord, my God, I take refuge in you.

READING   (Matthew 7:7-11)
Ask and you will receive. Seek and you will find. Knock and it will be opened to you. For the one who asks receives. The one who seeks finds. The one who knocks enters. Would one of you hand his son a stone when he asks for a loaf, or a poisonous snake when he asks for a fish? If you with all your sins know how to give your children what is good, how much more will your heavenly Father give good things to anyone who asks him!

SILENCE/SHARING

CLOSING HYMN

## PRAYER CORNER

### THEME: FORGIVENESS

**OPENING HYMN**

**OPENING PRAYER**   God of kindness and love, you always hear my prayer. I ask you to free me from all sin and evil. I am sorry for ever having hurt my brothers and sisters in word or deed. Forgive me for every wrong I may have ever committed in my entire life. Strengthen me from now on to act lovingly toward everyone. I ask this in Jesus' name. Amen.

**PSALM**   (All) Have mercy on me, O God, have mercy.

(Leader) Have mercy on me, O God, in your goodness; in the greatness of your compassion wipe out my offense. Thoroughly wash me from my guilt and of my sin cleanse me.

(All) Have mercy on me, O God, have mercy.

**READING**   (Matthew 6:9-15)
This is how you are to pray: Our Father in heaven, hallowed be your name, your kingdom come, your will be done on earth as it is in heaven. Give us today our daily bread, and forgive us the wrong we have done as we forgive those who wrong us. Subject us not to the trial but deliver us from the evil one. If you forgive the faults of others, your heavenly Father will forgive you yours. If you do not forgive others, neither will your Father forgive you.

**SILENCE/SHARING**

**CLOSING HYMN**

# PRAYER CORNER

## *THEME: CHRISTMAS*

**OPENING HYMN**

**OPENING PRAYER**  Come, Lord Jesus, do not delay; give new courage to your people who trust in your love. By your coming, raise us to the joy of your kingdom.

**PSALM**  (All) I will sing forever of your love, O Lord.

(Leader) I will sing forever of your love, O Lord; through all ages my mouth will proclaim your truth. Of this I am sure, that your love lasts forever, that your truth is firmly established as the heavens.

(All) I will sing forever of your love, O Lord.

**READING**  (Luke 1:26-38)
In the sixth month the angel Gabriel was sent by God to a town in Galilee called Nazareth, to a virgin betrothed to a man named Joseph, of the house of David; and the virgin's name was Mary. He went in and said to her, "Rejoice, so highly favored! The Lord is with you."

"I am the handmaid of the Lord," said Mary; "let what you have said be done to me." And the angel left her.

**SILENCE/SHARING**

**CLOSING HYMN**

# Conclusion

The preceding chapters expose some though not all of the service programs successfully implemented in a large Queens, New York parish. Any one of these programs can be independently created and implemented with relative ease. When programs multiply, however, the work of the Outreach director becomes increasingly challenging, making remembering and organizing impractical or even impossible. In such cases a triage form becomes a saving tool. This form focuses on the need of a caller or presenter and it smoothly channels the person to the appropriate parish program or services. Some examples will help to clarify.

Example A: a person calls or presents himself or herself as a potential Outreach volunteer. A triage form is completed in the Outreach office or in the rectory proper. The Outreach director receives this form and arranges an interview with the volunteer. Depending upon the program preference of the volunteer, the appropriate Outreach program form is then completed, e.g., the volunteer preference form (page 97) or the volunteer information form (page 61).

Example B: someone calls or presents himself or herself in need of food. A triage form is completed. An arrangement is made to interview (counseling and referral program) the presenter or caller. Following the counseling and referral assessment, this person, if accepted, is registered for the food distribution program, using the food program registration form (page 91). The triage form can then be attached to the narrative form of the counseling and referral program (pages 77-78), thus becoming the intake tool for counseling and referral record keeping.

Thus the triage form simplifies organization and is used to systematize and channel all requests for Outreach assistance.

While Outreach coordinators may be excellent program leaders, the director has the indispensable role of organizing and synchronizing, integrating and overseeing, all Outreach volunteers and programs. It is the director who interweaves programs and interprets policies. As pace-setter, model, and animator of compassion, the role of the director cannot be denied or supplanted.

# OUTREACH
## *TRIAGE FORM*

Name _____ Date _____

Address _____ Telephone _____

           ____ Needs Help       ____ "Walk-In"

           ____ Wants to Volunteer       ____ Telephoned

*Areas of Interest/Concern:*

____ Homebound (If the person is calling out of *need* please complete box)

---

Referred by:  Name _____  Relationship_____

                    Telephone _____

---

     ____ Food Program     ____ Child Care     ____ Flower Ministry

     ____ Bereavement     ____ Shelter     ____ Employment

     ____ Other (explain below)

Additional Information/Comments:_____

_____

_____

_____

_____

_____

_____

_____

Signature of Intake Person: _____

# Epilogue

Hopefully this book has assisted you the reader to reexamine and focus on your own personal resources and those of your worshiping community toward benefiting "the neighbor" among you. It is important to point out that many people who become volunteers in parish Outreach programs become catechized through the service given to their neighbor. Outreach's pastoral approach to people seems to be the inverse of tradition where service is born out of worship and prayer. For many Outreach volunteers, serving the neighbor is their "prayer," their initial contact with and discovery of God. Outreach volunteers include the alienated and unchurched as well as faithful parishioners. For the former it is generally "the neighbor" who points them to God, while the latter usually come to define and assist "the neighbor" through their participation in the life of the church.

Spiritually wounded good Samaritans compassionately binding the various wounds of the needy neighbor is mutual catechesis in action. Parish Outreach makes the church's social message viable and credible "more from the witness of actions than as a result of internal logic and consistency" (*Centesimus Annus*, John Paul II).